The Slow Cooker Bible

pil

Publications International, Ltd.

Pictured on the front cover *(top to bottom):* Easy Homemade Barbecue Sandwiches *(page 112)* and Pot Roast *(page 64).*

Pictured on the back cover *(clockwise from top):* Honey-Mustard Chicken Wings *(page 26),* Cherry Flan *(page 244)* and Chili *(page 178).*

ISBN-13: 978-1-4508-2177-3
ISBN-10: 1-4508-2177-4

Library of Congress Control Number: 2005927784

Manufactured in China.

8 7 6 5 4 3 2 1

Microwave Cooking: Microwave ovens vary in wattage. Use the cooking times as guidelines and check for doneness before adding more time.

Preparation/Cooking Times: Preparation times are based on the approximate amount of time required to assemble the recipe before cooking, baking, chilling or serving. These times include preparation steps such as measuring, chopping and mixing. The fact that some preparations and cooking can be done simultaneously is taken into account. Preparation of optional ingredients and serving suggestions is not included.

Publications International, Ltd.

contents

The Joy of Slow Cooking

The slow cooker is one of the most popular appliances in today's kitchen—and for good reason. What other appliance allows you to start dinner in the morning, then gives you the freedom to enjoy your day far from your kitchen? And, when you arrive home, a hot savory dinner is waiting. You can easily take a slow-cooked dinner to a potluck supper and keep it warm during serving. When entertaining, you can rely on your slow cooker to free up a burner or leave valuable oven space for another item on your menu. Plus, cleanup is quick and easy. No wonder slow cookers are loved by cooks across America.

The information that follows is designed to help you get the most from your slow cooker. You'll learn what they do best and why. Discover important techniques that can produce more flavorful dishes or help you create low-fat meals. Learn the tricks to cooking rice, pasta, fish and baked goods like cakes and breads. And you'll understand how to safely prepare foods at home and transport them. Finally, this book is packed with more than 270 taste-tempting recipes your family is sure to love. From easy appetizers and hearty main dishes to hot soups, spicy chilis and even desserts, this book has a fabulous collection of winning recipes and valuable information.

Don't wait any longer to get started on a quick course in slow cooking. Soon you'll be putting all your new knowledge to work to prepare family-pleasing meals every day of the week.

Slow Cooker Basics

A Little Bit of History

The introduction of the slow cooker: The first electric slow cooker was introduced in 1971. It was a more versatile variation of an electric bean pot. Available in only one size, 2½ quarts, it was similar in appearance and operation to today's models.

In the 1960's, women in the United States were joining the work force in huge numbers; for the first time family cooks were away from home many days of the week. It suddenly became important to find ways to quickly get dinner on the table after work. The maker of the first slow cooker saw the need and responded with an appliance that surprisingly didn't prepare dinner quickly, but rather it cooked dinner slowly while the cook was off pursuing her career. When the energy crisis occurred not long afterward, sales skyrocketed. The energy-efficient slow cooker was a huge hit.

The rebirth of the slow cooker: After its first brush with popularity, the slow cooker lost favor as other options were presented to cooks. A variety of frozen and shelf-stable meals became available and fast food restaurants multiplied. Although its popularity waned, a group of determined home cooks continued to love the appliance and used it frequently. In the mid 1990's the slow cooker began a slow comeback, aided by the introduction of slow cooker cookbooks with contemporary recipes. With their newly found popularity, slow cookers began to appear in more and more kitchens, at potluck suppers and on buffet tables. Manufacturers responded with variations on the original slow cooker: more sizes, more features and more creative ways to use them.

Popularity: Slow cookers remain popular in the twenty-first century for many reasons. First and foremost, they are easy and convenient to use. The concept is simple: cooking slowly at a temperature high enough for food safety but low enough that the cook doesn't need to attend to it for long periods of time. Busy cooks appreciate one-dish meals because they require little attention, cleanup is quick and everyone loves the food.

How Does It Work?

Basic concept: A slow cooker is usually a metal container with a heavy ceramic insert. Inserts have either a clear glass or plastic cover. Most inserts are removable for easy cleaning.

There are two general types of slow cookers. The most common type has heating coils that circle the outer container, producing heat on either a low or high setting. The low setting is generally about 200°F and the high setting is about 300°F. Food is placed in the insert, covered and heated by the slow steady heat produced by the coils. The recipes in this book were developed and tested with this type of slow cooker. The second type has heating coils under the insert that cycle on and off. The recipes in this book have not been tested with this type of appliance, so refer to the manufacturer's directions for help.

The slow cooking process creates steam. Since the slow cooker is covered throughout the cooking process, the steam can't escape. Instead, it condenses to form liquid that returns to the food. The amount of liquid in the food increases during cooking, so don't be surprised if there doesn't seem to be enough liquid when you begin cooking.

Slow cookers require very little energy, making them economical to use. In addition, they don't heat the kitchen, so they are a good choice for cooking on hot summer days.

What they do best: Slow cookers are ideal for making soups, stews and chilis and dishes that require long cooking. Slow cooking allows flavors of the meat or poultry and vegetables to develop and blend. Long slow cooking tenderizes meat. Choosing less tender cuts of meat is wise and you'll save money because tougher cuts are often more economical.

Other uses: Slow cookers are useful when entertaining. When used to prepare one of the dishes on the menu, a slow cooker will free up a burner or space in the oven for something else. And the slow-cooked dish gives you more time to concentrate on other menu items. A slow cooker can also be used to keep foods hot on a buffet table. Whether it's hot mulled cider, a warm artichoke dip or a main dish, your slow cooker can save the day.

Prepare your favorite slow-cooked dish and carry it to a potluck dinner. (Special carriers are made for just this purpose.) Desserts, such as fruit dishes, puddings and custards, can be prepared in a slow cooker. Surprisingly, even cakes can be made in this appliance. You'll find that these cakes are moist because they've been steamed. They can be made right in the ceramic insert or any oven-safe pan that fits your slow cooker. Pudding cakes, moist cakes with pudding underneath, also work well in a slow cooker.

Don't try this at home: Since a slow cooker uses low temperatures, it can't be used for sautéing or deep frying. Nor can it be used to cook a large quantity of pasta. Leftovers should never be reheated in a slow cooker. For safety's sake, leftovers need to be reheated quickly (see Slow Cooker Safety, page 19 for more information).

There are electric cookers available that do many things besides slow cooking. If you're looking for greater versatility in one appliance—steaming, boiling, deep frying and slow cooking—do research at a retail dealer that carries small appliances or on the Internet. These units have heating coils on the bottom of the unit. The recipes in this book have not been tested in this type of unit, so rely on the manufacturer's directions to guide you.

Choosing a Slow Cooker

It's important to know how you plan to use a slow cooker before shopping for one. For everyday cooking, choose a size large enough to serve your family (see the chart below). If you plan

to use the slow cooker primarily for entertaining, choose one of the larger sizes. The 16-ounce size is great for keeping dips warm. This unit has only one heat setting, low. If you're new to slow cooking, consider choosing a basic unit. They can be found for under $20 at discount stores. You can always upgrade later. Some cooks find owning more than one slow cooker useful.

Sizes: Basic slow cookers range in size from 16 ounces to 6½ quarts; they can be either round or oval in shape. Round slow cookers are more common and generally less expensive; oval units can more easily accommodate large pieces of meat. Choose the appropriate size from the chart above. Most recipes in this book require a 2½- to 3½-quart slow cooker.

Slow cooker size	Number of servings
16 ounces	1 to 2
1½ quarts	1 to 2
2½ quarts	2 to 4
3 quarts	3 to 4
3½ quarts	3 to 5
4 quarts	4 to 6
5 quarts	4 to 6
6½ quarts	6 to 8

Features: Features available on some slow cookers include keep-warm settings, programmable timers, delayed-start settings, fast-start settings and countdown timers. There's even a model that has preprogrammed settings for a host of specific recipes. If you need even greater flexibility than most slow cookers, look for a unit with a ceramic insert that has been designed to handle extreme temperatures; the insert can be used on the range top and in the oven. Keep in mind that the more features a model has, the higher the price.

Extras: Accessories for slow cookers include travel carriers, storage covers, meat racks and baking pans.

Slow Cooker Techniques

If you have never used a slow cooker, the following techniques will help you get started and give you a clear understanding of the world of slow cooking. If you're an old hand at slow cooking, browse through the list of techniques and you might find the solution to a problem you've experienced. Or you might discover something new that will enhance your slow-cooking experience and turn you into an expert.

Tenderizing: Since slow cooking is an effective way to tenderize meat, tougher cuts that have more flavor than lean cuts are an excellent choice. Many of the recipes in the "Hearty Meat Dishes" chapter include cuts like chuck roast, rump roast, stew meat, pork spareribs and pork shoulder. But the selection isn't limited to just these cuts; you'll find some of the convenient choices you love, such as flank steak, ground beef, sausage and pork chops.

Preparing meat: It is best to trim meat and poultry of excess fat before cooking, because the fat will liquefy and float to the top and you'll need to skim it off after cooking. You may wish to brown meat in a skillet before adding it to the slow cooker.

Browning: While not necessary, browning meat does have benefits. You've probably noticed that searing meat on a grill or in a skillet produces wonderful aromas and distinctive flavors that make steaks, burgers and chops extra special. The flavor produced by browning will add complexity to slow-cooked beef, pork and lamb meals. Ground meat should always be browned and drained of fat before placing it in the slow cooker. Browning also gives meat a more pleasant color.

Preparing poultry: Chicken skin tends to shrivel and curl in the slow cooker, so most recipes call for skinless chicken. If you prefer to use skin-on pieces, brown them in a skillet before adding them to the slow cooker. Remove excess fat from poultry before cooking it. A whole chicken is too large to cook safely in a slow cooker; always cut whole chickens into quarters or individual pieces before cooking.

You can purchase skin-on chicken for greater savings. To remove the skin, simply grasp the skin using a paper towel and pull it away from the meat.

Preparing vegetables: Vegetables, especially root vegetables, can take longer to cook than meats. Cut vegetables into uniform pieces so they finish cooking at the same time. Root vegetables, like potatoes, carrots and

turnips, should be cut into small pieces and placed on the bottom of the slow cooker so they are always covered with liquid. Vegetables should not be precooked. Occasionally a recipe will call for sautéing onions and garlic; this is usually done to reduce their sharpness. For example, in Classic French Onion Soup (page 150), the onions are sautéed for 15 minutes to allow them to develop a caramelized flavor, which adds a very distinctive note to the finished soup.

Strong-flavored vegetables, such as broccoli, cabbage and cauliflower, should be added during the last hour or two of cooking. Shorter cooking prevents their flavor from overwhelming the dish. Tender, delicate vegetables, such as spinach, green onions and snow peas, should also be added during the last hour of cooking to prevent overcooking them.

Dairy products: Long, slow cooking (6 hours or more) can make dairy products curdle or separate. Add milk, cream, sour cream and cheese during the last 15 to 30 minutes of cooking.

Certain dairy products can be used successfully during long cooking because they have undergone high heat processing. Examples of these are processed cheese and evaporated milk, which can be safely added early in the cooking process. Condensed soups can also withstand long cooking.

Boosting flavor: When foods cook for a long time, dried herbs and some spices tend to diminish in flavor, resulting in a bland dish. As more steam condenses in the slow cooker and the liquid in the dish increases, flavors become diluted. (Conventional cooking, on the other hand, results in evaporation of liquid and seasonings tend to become stronger the longer they are cooked.) To correct this problem, always taste the dish about 30 minutes before the end of the cooking time and add additional herbs and spices as needed.

On the other hand, some spices and garlic increase in flavor. The best examples of this are chiles, chili powder and pepper, which can become very harsh and extra spicy during long cooking. If you or a family member is sensitive to heat from chiles and spices, use less than the recipe suggests or wait until the last 30 minutes to add them.

The flavors of fresh herbs will increase during long cooking, making fresh herbs a good choice for slow cooking.

Improving color: Long cooking can result in vegetables losing their bright color. Finished dishes may look washed out. To avoid this problem, add delicate vegetables near the end of cooking. Another option is to garnish the dish before serving. Colorful garnishes like chopped green onions, chopped herbs, chopped fresh tomatoes, shredded cheese, lemon or lime wedges, and crisply cooked and crumbled bacon add just the special touch needed. Sour cream, toasted nuts and croutons also add interest. Be sure that the flavor of the garnish complements rather than detracts from the dish.

Make-ahead preparation: Mornings can be hectic times. If time is at a premium in the morning in your kitchen, you may find it easier to prepare ingredients the night before. For safety's sake, cover and refrigerate all items until ready to use. Also, keep vegetables in a separate bowl from raw meat and poultry. Do not brown meat or poultry the night before; partially cooking meat or poultry and refrigerating it allows bacteria to grow. Add the prepared ingredients to the slow cooker; you may need to add an extra 30 minutes to the cooking time because the ingredients will be very cold.

Filling the slow cooker: For best results, fill the slow cooker insert at least half full, but not more than three-quarters full. Many recipes recommend placing firm root vegetables on the bottom of the insert and the meat on top of the vegetables.

High versus low: Slow cookers have two settings, low and high. Most recipes can be cooked at either setting. Generally, 2 to 2½ hours on low equals 1 hour on high. Most of the recipes in this book give cooking times for both low and high settings. If the recipe only

lists one heat setting, this is the only one that should be used. Cooking on the low setting may result in slightly better blending of flavors and tough meats may become more tender when cooked on the low setting.

Start high, finish low: Another option for slow cooking is to cook for the first hour on the high setting, then reduce the heat to low to finish the dish. This reduces the total cooking time by one to two hours. Some slow cooker models offer a feature that automatically changes the heat setting to low after 1 hour on high.

Keep the lid on: A slow cooker can take as long as 30 minutes to regain the heat lost when the cover is removed during cooking. Only remove the cover when instructed to do so in the recipe. Generally, slow cooker dishes seldom, if ever, need stirring. With heating coils wrapped around the outside of the appliance and low heat, there's no danger of scorched food.

If you can't resist the urge to peek in the slow cooker, simply tap the cover gently or spin it lightly to remove some of the condensation. You should be able to see what's going on in the slow cooker.

Thickening: Thickeners are usually added during the last 15 to 30 minutes of cooking. The amount of liquid created in a slow cooker dish may vary from unit to unit. Cooking on the low heat setting or for a longer time results in more juices than cooking on high. Removing the lid repeatedly during cooking will reduce liquids. If there doesn't seem to be much liquid, use only a portion (one-half to three-fourths of the listed amount) of the thickening agent, adding more if necessary. If the sauce becomes too thick, simply thin it with additional broth or water.

There are four thickening agents that can be used in slow cookers. The two most common are flour and cornstarch.

Flour: All-purpose flour is most often used in the recipes in this book. Place the flour in a small bowl or cup and stir in enough cold water to make a thin, lump-free mixture; a whisk can help eliminate lumps. With the slow cooker on the high setting, quickly stir the flour mixture into the liquid in the slow cooker. (Remove large pieces of meat or poultry from the slow cooker before thickening the liquid.) Cook, stirring frequently, until the mixture thickens. Instant flour may be

substituted; it can be stirred directly into hot liquid.

Cornstarch: Cornstarch gives sauces a clear, shiny appearance; it is used most often for sweet dessert sauces and stir-fry sauces. Place the cornstarch in a small bowl or cup and stir in cold water, stirring until the cornstarch dissolves. Quickly stir this mixture into the liquid in the slow cooker; the sauce will thicken as soon as the liquid boils. Cornstarch breaks down with too much heat, so never add it at the beginning of the slow cooking process. And as soon as the sauce thickens, turn off the heat.

Arrowroot: Arrowroot (or arrowroot flour) is a ground powder of a tropical root; it produces a clear sauce. Those who are allergic to wheat often use it in place of flour. Place arrowroot in a small bowl or cup and stir in cold water until the mixture is smooth. Quickly stir this mixture into the liquid in the slow cooker. Unlike cornstarch, arrowroot thickens below the boiling point so it can thicken sauces easily with the low heat of a slow cooker. Too much stirring can break down an arrowroot mixture, so be sure and use it just before serving. (See the Substitution Guide on page 23 for information on substituting arrowroot for flour.)

Tapioca: Tapioca is a starchy substance extracted from the root of the cassava plant. It comes in many forms but it is the quick-cooking form that is used in several recipes in this book. Its greatest advantage is that it withstands long cooking, making it an ideal choice for slow cooking. Add it at the beginning of cooking and you'll get a clear thickened sauce in the finished dish. Dishes with tapioca as a thickener are best cooked on the low setting; tapioca may become stringy when boiled for a long time.

Low-fat techniques: One great advantage of slow cookers is that you can easily prepare low-fat meals in them. Since foods are not generally sautéed in butter or oil, the fat content is naturally lower in slow cooked meals. To trim even more fat from slow cooker dishes, choose lean meat, trim excess fat, remove the skin from chicken and brown meat in a nonstick skillet lightly sprayed with nonstick cooking spray. Or slip meat under the broiler for a few minutes to brown it before adding it to the slow

cooker. Any fat that does accumulate during cooking will rise to the surface and can be skimmed off.

Baked goods in a slow cooker: If you wish to prepare bread, cakes or pudding cakes in a slow cooker, you may want to purchase a covered, vented metal cake pan accessory for your slow cooker. You can also use any straight-sided soufflé dish or deep cake pan that will fit into the ceramic insert of your unit. Baked goods can be prepared directly in the insert; they can be a little

difficult to remove from the insert, so follow the recipe directions carefully. (See foil handles technique for tips on removing soufflé dishes and cake pans from your slow cooker.)

Doubling recipes: Generally, when doubling a recipe, double the amount of meat, vegetables, herbs and spices. (See page 11 for spices that increase in flavor; don't double these. Instead, make adjustments near the end of the cooking time.) Only increase liquid ingredients by 50 percent. Refer to your owner's manual for additional instructions.

High altitude adjustments: If you live at an altitude above 3500 feet, you will need to make some adjustments when slow cooking. Everything will take longer to cook, so plan for that. Tough meats take longer to tenderize at high altitudes, sometimes much longer; try cooking on the high heat setting instead of low. Root vegetables take longer to cook as well; cut them into smaller pieces than the recipe suggests for quicker cooking.

Foil handles: To easily lift a dish or a meat loaf from a slow cooker, make foil handles as follows.

Tear off three 18×3-inch strips of heavy-duty foil. Crisscross the strips so they resemble the spokes of a wheel. Place the dish of food in the center of the strips.

Pull the strips up and over the dish or food; using the foil handles, lift and place it into the slow cooker. Leave the strips in during cooking so you can easily lift the dish or food out again when it is ready.

Slow Cooker Techniques for Special Foods

Frozen foods: Avoid cooking frozen foods in a slow cooker. For food safety's sake, do not cook frozen meat or chicken in a slow cooker. Instead, thaw it in the refrigerator before cooking. It's best not to cook packages of frozen vegetables in a slow cooker; rather, thaw them or cook them conventionally or in a microwave oven. You may add small amounts (½ to 1 cup) of frozen vegetables, such as peas, green beans, broccoli florets and corn, to a slow-cooked meal during the last 30 to 45 minutes of cooking. Cook on the high setting until the vegetables are tender. (You may need to add a few minutes to the cooking time.)

Rice: Choose converted long-grain rice (or arborio rice when suggested) or wild rice for best results. Long, slow cooking can turn other types of rice into mush; if you prefer to use other types of rice instead of converted rice, cook them conventionally and add them to the slow cooker during the last 15 minutes of cooking. You can add a small amount (½ cup) of uncooked rice to a slow cooker soup or other dish; be sure to add it to boiling liquid during the last

hour of cooking and cook on the high setting. (You may need to add a few minutes to the cooking time.)

If you wish to add rice to a recipe that doesn't include it, you will need to adjust the liquid as well. Add an equal amount of broth or water before you add the rice.

Pasta: Pasta needs to be cooked in a large quantity of boiling water; it should not be cooked in a slow cooker. However, you can add small amounts (½ to 1 cup) of small pasta, such as orzo, small shell macaroni, ditali and short lengths of linguine to boiling liquid during the last hour of slow cooking. You may also cook pasta in boiling water

and add it to the slow cooker during the last 30 minutes of cooking.

Fish: Fish cooks quickly and can easily be overcooked. That's why it requires special care when slow cooking. First, choose only firm white fish, such as cod, haddock, sea bass, red snapper or orange roughy. Avoid more delicate varieties and thin fillets because they will fall apart. If fish is frozen, thaw it overnight in its original packaging before cooking it.

Add the fish 30 to 45 minutes before the end of the cooking time. Change the heat setting to high before you add the fish, cover the slow cooker and cook until the fish just begins to flake when tested with a fork. The cooking time is dependent upon the quantity and the thickness of the fillets—the thicker the fillets and the more of them, the longer they take to cook.

Shellfish: Shellfish, such as shrimp, are delicate and should be added to the slow cooker during the last 15 to 30 minutes of the cooking time. Always use a high heat setting for shellfish. If you add a large quantity of shellfish to the slow cooker, you may need to add a little extra cooking time. Watch shellfish carefully; it overcooks easily.

Dried beans: It's best to presoak dried beans before cooking them in a slow cooker. This softens them and gives them a head start on cooking. Softening beans reduces the cooking time. (Lentils and split peas do not need to be softened.) The two methods for presoaking follow:

Traditional method: Place dried beans that have been sorted and rinsed in a bowl. Cover them with cold, unsalted water and let them stand overnight. Drain off the water and place the beans in the slow cooker.

Quick method: Place sorted and rinsed beans in a large saucepan; cover them with twice their volume of cold unsalted water. Bring the water to a boil over high heat. Boil for 2 minutes. Remove the saucepan from the heat, cover it and let it stand for 1 hour. Drain off the water and place the beans in the slow cooker.

Even when beans are presoaked, they take a long time to cook. Avoid adding acids or sweeteners to the beans until they are soft. Acids and sweeteners will slow down the softening process and will lengthen the cooking time. Acids include tomatoes, vinegar and citrus juices. Sweeteners include sugar, honey and molasses. Add these items toward the end of the cooking time.

Fondue: A small slow cooker (1½ quarts) makes a perfect stand-in for a fondue pot. Whether you want to make a cheese fondue or a chocolate dessert fondue, the low heat of a slow cooker ensures perfectly melted cheese or chocolate in 45 minutes to 1 hour.

Adapting Recipes to the Slow Life

You can adapt many of your favorite conventional recipes to the slow cooker. Choose recipes that are normally prepared on top of the stove, such as soups, stews, chilis and braised meats and poultry; they tend to adapt better. Find a similar slow cooker recipe to use as a guide. Note the cooking times, amount of liquid, quantity and size of meat and vegetable pieces. Because the slow cooker captures moisture during cooking, you will want to reduce the amount of liquid by one-third to half.

Follow the techniques suggested in the previous pages for meat, poultry, vegetables, cheese, rice, pasta, seasoning and thickening. Make sure the slow cooker is at least half full

If your converted recipe has too much liquid, you can scoop out the excess and discard it. Or you can remove the excess and place it in a saucepan; simmer it until the mixture is reduced by at least half. This technique is called "reducing," which reduces the liquid while intensifying flavors. Add the reduced liquid back to the slow cooker.

(see page 12). You may find you need to experiment a little to get the proportions correct.

Caring for Slow Cookers

Cleaning: Cleaning your slow cooker is actually pretty simple. Refer to the tips that follow for basic guidelines.

- Always wash a new ceramic insert in hot sudsy water before cooking in it. It may have a film on it from the manufacturing process.

- For sticky foods like barbecued ribs and other foods containing sugary ingredients, spray the insert with nonstick cooking spray for easier cleanup.

- After cooking, wash the cool insert in hot sudsy water.

- To remove any sticky food, soak the insert in hot sudsy water, then scrub it with a plastic or nylon scrubber. Do not use steel wool.

- Wipe the cool outer container with a damp cloth.

Extreme temperatures: Ceramic inserts are sensitive to sudden changes in temperature. Don't place a cold ceramic insert into a preheated base. Don't place a hot insert on a cold surface, in the refrigerator or fill it with cold water. Unless the manufacturer's directions say you can use the ceramic insert in a conventional or microwave oven, don't. Finally, never place the ceramic insert in the freezer.

Slow Cooker Safety

Food safety: Food safety is always a concern when you're cooking and serving food. Organisms that cause foodborne illness thrive at temperatures between 40°F and 140°F. Research has shown that slow cookers, even on the low heat setting, raise the temperature of the food quickly through this danger zone, making them a safe way to cook.

Power outage: If you arrive home and find the electrical power service to your home is out, check the slow cooker immediately. With an instant-read thermometer, check the temperature of the contents of the slow cooker. If the temperature is above 140°F, you can transfer the contents to a large saucepan or Dutch oven and finish cooking it

on a range or grill. However, if the temperature of the contents is between 40° and 140°F, you should throw the contents away.

If the electricity is on when you arrive home, but you can tell by the clocks that your home has been without power, the best thing to do is throw away the food. You will never know what the temperature of the food was when the power went off or how long it was off; the food may have spent several hours in the danger zone. And, although the food is hot when you get home and looks done, it is better to err on the side of safety and throw it away.

Make-ahead safety: When you prepare ingredients ahead for later cooking, always refrigerate meat and vegetables. Store raw meat and poultry in a separate bowl from the vegetables. Do not store ingredients in the slow cooker insert; starting with a cold insert will lengthen the cooking time.

Frozen foods: Do not cook frozen meat or poultry in the slow cooker. It takes too long on either the low or high setting to go through the danger zone, which gives organisms a perfect place to grow and multiply. Frozen vegetables are best prepared on the range top or in a microwave oven.

Browning: Never brown or partially cook meat or poultry, then refrigerate it for later cooking. Instead, cook it immediately after browning.

Cook meat and poultry thoroughly: At the end of the cooking time, check the temperatures of poultry, meat and meat loaf using an instant read thermometer. Poultry should be 165°F, beef and pork 160° to 170°F and meat loaf 165°F.

Warm setting: Some slow cookers have a warm setting that is designed to hold food above 165°F. You can confirm that your slow cooker is working properly by checking the temperature of the food periodically while it is on the warm setting. The temperature should not drop below 140°F.

Leftovers: Refrigerate leftovers quickly. Food can stand in a slow cooker that is turned off for up to 1 hour. To quickly chill leftovers, divide them into several small containers rather than one large container; they will chill faster and bacteria will have less chance to multiply. Never reheat leftovers in a slow cooker. Instead, heat them quickly on the top of the range or in a microwave oven.

Filling the slow cooker: A slow cooker that is less than half full may not heat food quickly enough. Since the heating coils circle the outer container, most of the food will not be in contact with the heat source.

Appliance safety: Slow cookers are safe to leave unattended while they are cooking. If you plan to be away from the house all day, it is safer to leave the slow cooker on the low setting. Do not use your slow cooker near the kitchen sink. Choose an electrical outlet

at least three feet from the sink. Never immerse the base unit in water. Do not use the ceramic insert if it is cracked; replace it. For further safety tips, refer to the manufacturer's instructions.

Electrical cords: Protect the electrical cord from nicks and cuts. Check the cord periodically; if you find nicks or cuts in the cord, replace it. Do not use an extension cord with a slow cooker.

Slow Cooker Pantry

A well-stocked pantry can make slow cooking even more convenient. Having frequently used items on hand means you can prepare dinner without a special trip to the supermarket. The following items are often used in slow cooker recipes. Customize the list so you can prepare your favorite recipes any time.

Canned chicken and beef broth	Pasta	Brown sugar
Condensed cream soups	Converted long-grain rice	All-purpose flour
Canned diced tomatoes	Dried herbs	Cornstarch or arrowroot
Tomato sauce	Vegetable oil	Evaporated milk
Tomato paste	Olive oil	Onions
Dried beans	Nonstick cooking spray	Garlic
Canned beans	Granulated sugar	Boiling potatoes

Keep your refrigerator stocked with your favorite slow cooker vegetables and dairy products.

Carrots

Celery

Bell peppers

Milk

Sour cream

Cheese

Keep a small assortment of frozen meat, poultry and vegetables in the freezer.

Lean ground beef* (1-pound packages)

Beef stew meat* (1-pound packages)

Chicken pieces* (packages of 4 pieces)

Boneless chicken breasts* (packages of 2 breasts)

Green peas

Green beans

Corn

Stew vegetables

*Meat and poultry have limited storage time in the freezer. Use ground beef within 3 months, stew meat within 6 months and poultry within 8 months. If you don't use these packages of meat and poultry for slow-cooked meals, be sure and use them for something else before they lose quality. Always thaw meat, poultry and large quantities of vegetables before cooking them in a slow cooker (see "Frozen foods" page 16).

Ingredient Substitution Guide

If you don't have:	Use:
Arrowroot (1 tablespoon)	2½ tablespoons all-purpose flour
Baking powder (1 teaspoon)	¼ teaspoon baking soda plus ½ teaspoon cream of tartar
Bread crumbs (1 cup)	1 cup cracker crumbs
Broth, chicken or beef (1 cup)	1 bouillon cube or ½ teaspoon granules mixed with 1 cup boiling water
Butter (¼ cup or ½ stick)	¼ cup margarine or 3½ tablespoons vegetable oil
Cheddar cheese (1 cup shredded)	1 cup shredded Colby or Monterey Jack cheese
Cornstarch (1 tablespoon)	2 tablespoons all-purpose flour
Ricotta cheese (1 cup)	1 cup small curd cottage cheese
Cream or half-and-half (1 cup)	1½ tablespoons melted butter plus enough milk to equal 1 cup
Garlic (1 small clove)	⅛ teaspoon garlic powder or ¼ teaspoon garlic salt
Ketchup (1 cup)	1 cup tomato sauce plus 1 teaspoon vinegar and 1 tablespoon sugar
Lemon juice (1 teaspoon)	½ teaspoon vinegar or 1 teaspoon lime juice or white wine
Lemon or orange peel, fresh (1 teaspoon)	½ teaspoon dried peel
Mayonnaise (½ cup)	½ cup sour cream or plain yogurt
Milk, evaporated (1 cup)	1 cup light cream
Mushrooms, fresh (½ pound)	1 can (4 ounces) mushrooms
Mustard, prepared (1 tablespoon)	1 teaspoon dried mustard
Onions, minced (¼ cup)	1 tablespoon dry minced onion
Asiago or Romano cheese, grated (½ cup)	½ cup grated Parmesan cheese
Dried cranberries (1 cup)	1 cup raisins
Saffron threads (½ teaspoon)	½ teaspoon turmeric
Sour cream (1 cup)	1 cup plain yogurt (not low-fat)
Tomato juice (1 cup)	½ cup tomato sauce plus ½ cup water
Tomato sauce (1 cup)	⅜ cup (6 tablespoons) tomato paste plus ½ cup water
Vinegar (1 teaspoon)	2 teaspoons lemon or lime juice
Wine (1 cup)	1 cup chicken or beef broth or 1 cup fruit juice mixed with 2 teaspoons vinegar

Appetizers & Snacks

Chunky Pinto Bean Dip

2 cans (about 15 ounces each) pinto beans, rinsed and drained
1 can (about 14 ounces) diced tomatoes with green chiles, undrained
1 cup chopped onion
⅔ cup chunky salsa
1 tablespoon vegetable oil
1½ teaspoons minced garlic
1 teaspoon ground coriander
1 teaspoon ground cumin
1½ cups (6 ounces) shredded Mexican cheese blend or Cheddar cheese
¼ cup chopped cilantro
Blue corn or other tortilla chips
Assorted raw vegetables

1. Combine beans, tomatoes, onion, salsa, oil, garlic, coriander and cumin in slow cooker.

2. Cover; cook on LOW 5 to 6 hours or until onion is tender.

3. Partially mash bean mixture with potato masher. Stir in cheese and cilantro. Serve at room temperature with chips and vegetables. *Makes about 5 cups*

Prep Time: 12 minutes
Cook Time: 5 to 6 hours

Chunky Pinto Bean Dip

Honey-Mustard Chicken Wings

3 pounds chicken wings
1 teaspoon salt
1 teaspoon black pepper
½ cup honey
½ cup barbecue sauce
2 tablespoons spicy brown mustard
1 clove garlic, minced
4 thin lemon slices

1. Preheat broiler. Rinse chicken and pat dry. Cut off and discard wing tips. Cut each wing in half at joint. Place chicken on rack in broiler pan; season with salt and pepper.

2. Broil 4 to 5 inches from heat about 10 minutes or until browned, turning once. Transfer chicken to slow cooker. Combine honey, barbecue sauce, mustard and garlic in small bowl; mix well. Pour sauce over chicken wings. Top with lemon slices.

3. Cover; cook on LOW 4 to 5 hours. Remove and discard lemon slices. Serve wings with sauce.   *Makes about 24 appetizers*

Prep Time: 20 minutes
Cook Time: 4 to 5 hours

Helpful Hint

Browning chicken before cooking it in a slow cooker serves several purposes: browning contributes a pleasant flavor as well as color to the chicken wings.

Honey-Mustard Chicken Wings

Creamy Artichoke-Parmesan Dip

    2 cans (14 ounces each) artichoke hearts, drained and chopped
    2 cups (8 ounces) shredded mozzarella cheese
 1½ cups grated Parmesan cheese
 1½ cups mayonnaise
    ½ cup finely chopped onion
    ½ teaspoon dried oregano
    ¼ teaspoon garlic powder
    4 pita breads, cut into wedges
       Assorted cut-up vegetables

1. Combine artichokes, cheeses, mayonnaise, onion, oregano and garlic powder in slow cooker; mix well.

2. Cover; cook on LOW 2 hours. Arrange pita breads and vegetables on platter; serve with warm dip. *Makes 4 cups*

Cranberry-Barbecue Chicken Wings

    3 pounds chicken wings
       Salt and black pepper
    1 container (12 ounces) cranberry-orange relish
    ½ cup barbecue sauce
    2 tablespoons quick-cooking tapioca
    1 tablespoon prepared mustard
       Hot cooked rice (optional)

1. Preheat broiler. Rinse chicken and pat dry. Cut off and discard wing tips. Cut each wing in half at joint. Place chicken on rack in broiler pan; season with salt and pepper.

2. Broil 4 to 5 inches from heat 10 to 12 minutes or until browned, turning once. Transfer chicken to slow cooker. Stir relish, barbecue sauce, tapioca and mustard in small bowl. Pour over chicken.

3. Cover; cook on LOW 4 to 5 hours. Serve with hot cooked rice, if desired.
Makes about 16 appetizers

Creamy Artichoke-Parmesan Dip

Slow Cooker Cheese Dip

1 pound ground beef
1 pound bulk Italian sausage
1 package (16 ounces) pasteurized processed cheese spread, cubed
1 can (11 ounces) sliced jalapeño peppers, drained
2 cups (8 ounces) Cheddar cheese, cubed
1 medium onion, diced
1 package (8 ounces) cream cheese, cubed
1 container (8 ounces) cottage cheese
1 container (8 ounces) sour cream
1 can (about 8 ounces) diced tomatoes, drained
3 cloves garlic, minced
   Salt and black pepper
   Tortilla chips or crackers

1. Brown ground beef and sausage 6 to 8 minutes in medium skillet over medium-high heat, stirring to break up meat. Drain fat. Transfer to 4-quart slow cooker.

2. Add processed cheese, jalapeño peppers, Cheddar cheese, onion, cream cheese, cottage cheese, sour cream, tomatoes and garlic to slow cooker. Season with salt and black pepper.

3. Cover; cook on HIGH 1½ to 2 hours or until cheeses are melted. Serve with tortilla chips. *Makes 16 to 18 servings*

Helpful Hint

Processed cheese can better withstand long slow cooking. Since it is processed with heat and has emulsifiers added, it will remain smooth and creamy.

Slow Cooker Cheese Dip

Spicy Sweet & Sour Cocktail Franks

2 packages (8 ounces each) cocktail franks
½ cup ketchup or chili sauce
½ cup apricot preserves
1 teaspoon hot pepper sauce plus additional for serving

1. Combine cocktail franks, ketchup, preserves and hot pepper sauce in 1½-quart slow cooker; mix well.

2. Cover; cook on LOW 2 to 3 hours. Serve with cocktail picks and additional hot pepper sauce. *Makes about 4 dozen*

Chili con Queso

1 package (16 ounces) pasteurized processed cheese spread, cut into cubes
1 can (about 10 ounces) diced tomatoes with green chiles, undrained
1 cup sliced green onions
2 teaspoons *each* ground coriander and ground cumin
¾ teaspoon hot pepper sauce
Green onion strips and hot pepper slices (optional)
Tortilla chips

1. Combine cheese spread, tomatoes, green onions, coriander and cumin in slow cooker; stir until well blended.

2. Cover; cook on LOW 2 to 3 hours. Garnish with green onion strips and hot pepper slices. Serve with tortilla chips. *Makes 3 cups*

Serving Suggestion: For something different, cut pita bread into triangles and toast them in a preheated 400°F oven for 5 minutes or until they are crisp.

Spicy Sweet & Sour Cocktail Franks

Barbecued Meatballs

     2 pounds ground beef
1⅓ cups ketchup, divided
     3 tablespoons seasoned dry bread crumbs
     1 egg, lightly beaten
     2 tablespoons dried onion flakes
    ¾ teaspoon garlic salt
    ½ teaspoon black pepper
     1 cup packed light brown sugar
     1 can (6 ounces) tomato paste
    ¼ cup soy sauce
    ¼ cup cider vinegar
1½ teaspoons hot pepper sauce
     Diced bell peppers (optional)

1. Preheat oven to 350°F.

2. Combine ground beef, ⅓ cup ketchup, bread crumbs, egg, onion flakes, garlic salt and black pepper in medium bowl; mix thoroughly. Shape into 1-inch meatballs. Place meatballs in two 15×10-inch jelly-roll pans or shallow roasting pans.

3. Bake 18 minutes or until browned. Transfer meatballs to slow cooker. Mix remaining 1 cup ketchup, brown sugar, tomato paste, soy sauce, vinegar and hot pepper sauce in medium bowl. Pour over meatballs.

4. Cover; cook on LOW 4 hours. Serve with cocktail picks. Garnish with diced bell peppers. *Makes about 4 dozen*

Barbecued Franks: Arrange 2 (12-ounce) packages or 3 (8-ounce) packages cocktail franks in slow cooker. Combine 1 cup ketchup with brown sugar, tomato paste, soy sauce, vinegar and hot pepper sauce; pour over franks. Cook according to directions for Barbecued Meatballs.

Barbecued Meatballs

Parmesan Ranch Snack Mix

> 3 cups bite-size corn or rice cereal squares
> 2 cups oyster crackers
> 1 package (5 ounces) bagel chips, broken in half
> 1½ cups small pretzel twists
> 1 cup pistachio nuts
> 2 tablespoons grated Parmesan cheese
> ¼ cup (½ stick) butter, melted
> 1 package (1 ounce) dry ranch salad dressing mix
> ½ teaspoon garlic powder

1. Combine cereal, oyster crackers, bagel chips, pretzels, nuts and Parmesan cheese in slow cooker; mix gently. Combine butter, salad dressing mix and garlic powder in small bowl. Pour over cereal mixture; toss lightly to coat.

2. Cover; cook on LOW 3 hours. Remove cover; stir gently. Cook, uncovered, 30 minutes. Store snack mix in airtight container.   *Makes about 9½ cups*

Festive Bacon & Cheese Dip

> 2 packages (8 ounces each) cream cheese, cut into cubes
> 4 cups (16 ounces) shredded Colby-Jack cheese
> 1 cup half-and-half
> 2 tablespoons prepared mustard
> 1 tablespoon minced onion
> 2 teaspoons Worcestershire sauce
> ½ teaspoon salt
> ¼ teaspoon hot pepper sauce
> 1 pound bacon, crisp-cooked and crumbled
> Crusty bread or vegetable dippers

1. Combine cream cheese, Colby-Jack cheese, half-and-half, mustard, onion, Worcestershire sauce, salt and hot pepper sauce in slow cooker.

2. Cover; cook, stirring occasionally, on LOW 1 hour or until cheese is melted.

3. Stir in bacon; adjust seasonings. Serve with crusty bread.   *Makes about 4 cups*

Parmesan Ranch Snack Mix

Hearty Calico Bean Dip

¾ pound ground beef
½ pound sliced bacon, crisp-cooked and crumbled
1 can (about 16 ounces) baked beans
1 can (about 15 ounces) Great Northern beans, rinsed and drained
1 can (about 15 ounces) kidney beans, rinsed and drained
1 small onion, chopped
½ cup packed brown sugar
½ cup ketchup
1 tablespoon cider vinegar
1 teaspoon prepared yellow mustard
Tortilla chips

1. Brown beef 6 to 8 minutes in large nonstick skillet over medium-high heat, stirring to break up meat. Drain fat. Spoon meat into slow cooker. Add bacon, beans, onion, brown sugar, ketchup, vinegar and mustard to slow cooker; mix well.

2. Cover; cook on LOW 4 hours or on HIGH 2 hours. Serve with tortilla chips.

Makes 12 servings

Helpful Hint

Bacon can be easily cooked in a microwave oven. Simply place bacon strips without overlapping in a single layer between several layers of paper towels on a plate. Microwave about 1 minute per slice. Check for doneness three-fourths of the way through the cooking time. Cool bacon before crumbling.

Hearty Calico Bean Dip

Brats in Beer

1½ pounds bratwurst (about 5 or 6 links)
1 can or bottle (12 ounces) beer (not dark)
1 medium onion, thinly sliced
2 tablespoons packed brown sugar
2 tablespoons red wine or cider vinegar
Spicy brown mustard
Cocktail rye bread

1. Combine bratwurst, beer, onion, brown sugar and vinegar in slow cooker.

2. Cover; cook on LOW 4 to 5 hours.

3. Remove bratwurst from cooking liquid. Cut into ½-inch-thick slices. Spread mustard on cocktail rye bread; top with bratwurst slices and onions.

Makes 30 to 36 appetizers

Tip: Choose a light-tasting beer for cooking brats. Hearty ales might leave the meat tasting slightly bitter.

Curried Snack Mix

3 tablespoons butter
2 tablespoons packed light brown sugar
1½ teaspoons hot curry powder
¼ teaspoon salt
¼ teaspoon ground cumin
2 cups rice cereal squares
1 cup walnut halves
1 cup dried cranberries

1. Melt butter in large skillet. Add brown sugar, curry powder, salt and cumin; mix well. Add cereal, walnuts and cranberries; stir to coat. Transfer mixture to slow cooker.

2. Cover; cook on LOW 3 hours. Cook, uncovered, 30 minutes. Store snack mix in airtight container.

Makes 16 servings

Brats in Beer

Easy Taco Dip

½ pound ground beef chuck
1 cup frozen corn, thawed
½ cup chopped onion
½ cup salsa
½ cup mild taco sauce
1 can (4 ounces) diced mild green chiles
1 can (4 ounces) sliced ripe olives, drained
1 cup (4 ounces) shredded Mexican cheese blend
Tortilla chips
Sour cream

1. Brown beef 6 to 8 minutes in large nonstick skillet over medium-high heat, stirring to break up meat. Drain fat. Spoon into slow cooker.

2. Add corn, onion, salsa, taco sauce, chiles and olives to slow cooker; mix well. Cover; cook on LOW 2 to 3 hours.

3. Just before serving, stir in cheese. Serve with tortilla chips and sour cream.

Makes about 3 cups

Tip: To keep this dip hot through your entire party, simply leave it in the slow cooker on LOW or WARM.

Prep Time: 15 minutes
Cook Time: 2 to 4 hours

Easy Taco Dip

Party Mix

3 cups rice cereal squares
2 cups toasted oat cereal rings
2 cups bite-size shredded wheat cereal
1 cup pistachio nuts or peanuts
1 cup thin pretzel sticks
½ cup (1 stick) butter, melted
1 tablespoon Worcestershire sauce
1 teaspoon seasoned salt
½ teaspoon garlic powder

1. Combine cereals, nuts and pretzels in slow cooker. Mix butter, Worcestershire sauce, seasoned salt and garlic powder in small bowl. Pour over cereal mixture in slow cooker; toss lightly to coat.

2. Cover; cook on LOW 3 hours, stirring well every 30 minutes. Cook, uncovered, 30 minutes. Store in airtight container. *Makes 10 cups*

Creamy Cheesy Spinach Dip

2 packages (10 ounces each) frozen chopped spinach, thawed
2 cups chopped onions
1 teaspoon salt
½ teaspoon garlic powder
¼ teaspoon black pepper
12 ounces pasteurized processed cheese spread with jalapeño peppers, cubed
Assorted crackers (optional)
Cherry tomatoes with pulp removed (optional)

1. Drain spinach and squeeze dry, reserving ¾ cup liquid. Place spinach, reserved liquid, onions, salt, garlic powder and black pepper into 1½-quart slow cooker; stir to blend.

2. Cover; cook on HIGH 1½ hours. Stir in cheese and cook 30 minutes or until melted. Serve with crackers or fill cherry tomato shells. *Makes about 4 cups*

Tip: To thaw spinach quickly, remove paper wrapper from spinach containers. Microwave at HIGH 3 to 4 minutes or until just thawed.

Party Mix

Honey-Sauced Chicken Wings

        3 pounds chicken wings
        1 teaspoon salt
    ½ teaspoon black pepper
        1 cup honey
      ½ cup soy sauce
      ¼ cup chopped onion
      ¼ cup ketchup
        2 tablespoons vegetable oil
        2 cloves garlic, minced
      ¼ teaspoon red pepper flakes
            Toasted sesame seeds* (optional)

*To toast sesame seeds, spread in large, dry skillet. Shake skillet over medium-low heat about 3 minutes or until seeds begin to pop and turn golden.

1. Preheat broiler. Rinse chicken and pat dry. Cut off and discard wing tips. Cut each wing in half at joint. Place chicken on rack in broiler pan; season with salt and pepper.

2. Broil 4 to 5 inches from heat 20 minutes, turning once or until chicken is brown. Place chicken into slow cooker. Combine honey, soy sauce, onion, ketchup, oil, garlic and red pepper flakes in large bowl. Pour over chicken wings.

3. Cover; cook on LOW 4 to 5 hours or on HIGH 2 to 2½ hours. Garnish with sesame seeds.   *Makes about 32 appetizers*

Honey-Sauced Chicken Wings

Hearty Meat Dishes

Italian-Style Pot Roast

2 teaspoons minced garlic
1 teaspoon salt
1 teaspoon dried basil
1 teaspoon dried oregano
¼ teaspoon red pepper flakes
1 boneless beef bottom round rump or chuck shoulder roast (about 2½ to 3 pounds)
1 large onion, quartered and thinly sliced
1½ cups tomato-basil or marinara pasta sauce
2 cans (about 15 ounces each) cannellini or Great Northern beans, rinsed and drained
¼ cup shredded fresh basil or chopped Italian parsley

1. Combine garlic, salt, basil, oregano and red pepper flakes in small bowl; rub over roast. Place half of onion slices into slow cooker. Cut roast in half to fit into 4-quart slow cooker. Place one half of roast over onion slices; top with remaining onion slices and other half of roast. Pour pasta sauce over roast.

2. Cover; cook on LOW 8 to 9 hours or until roast is fork tender. Remove roast to cutting board; tent with foil. Let liquid in slow cooker stand 5 minutes to allow fat to rise. Skim off fat.

3. Stir beans into liquid. Cover; cook on HIGH 15 to 30 minutes or until beans are heated through. Carve roast across the grain into thin slices. Serve with bean mixture and fresh basil. *Makes 6 to 8 servings*

Prep Time: 15 minutes
Cook Time: 8 to 9 hours

Italian-Style Pot Roast

Broccoli and Beef Pasta

2 cups broccoli florets *or* 1 package (10 ounces) frozen broccoli, thawed
1 onion, thinly sliced
½ teaspoon dried basil
½ teaspoon dried oregano
½ teaspoon dried thyme
1 can (about 14 ounces) Italian-style diced tomatoes, undrained
¾ cup beef broth
1 pound ground beef
2 cloves garlic, minced
2 tablespoons tomato paste
2 cups cooked rotini pasta
¾ cup (3 ounces) shredded Cheddar cheese or grated Parmesan cheese, plus additional for garnish

1. Layer broccoli, onion, basil, oregano, thyme, tomatoes and broth in slow cooker. Cover; cook on LOW 2½ hours.

2. Brown beef and garlic 6 to 8 minutes in large nonstick skillet over medium-high heat, stirring to break up meat. Drain fat. Add beef mixture to slow cooker. Cover; cook 2 hours.

3. Stir in tomato paste, pasta and cheese. Cover; cook 30 minutes or until cheese melts and mixture is heated through. Sprinkle with additional shredded cheese.

Makes 4 servings

Serving Suggestion: Serve with garlic bread.

Broccoli and Beef Pasta

Chipotle Taco Filling

2 pounds ground beef
2 cups chopped yellow onions
2 cans (about 15 ounces each) pinto beans, rinsed and drained
1 can (about 14 ounces) diced tomatoes with peppers and onions, drained
2 chipotle peppers in adobo sauce, mashed
1 tablespoon beef bouillon granules
1 tablespoon sugar
1½ teaspoons ground cumin
Taco shells or flour tortillas
Toppings: shredded lettuce, salsa, shredded Cheddar cheese and sour cream

1. Brown beef 6 to 8 minutes in large nonstick skillet over medium-high heat, stirring to break up meat. Drain fat. Combine beef, onions, beans, tomatoes, chipotle peppers, bouillon, sugar and cumin in 3½- to 4-quart slow cooker.

2. Cover; cook on LOW 4 hours or on HIGH 2 hours. Serve filling in taco shells. Serve with desired toppings.

Makes 8 cups

Slow Cooker Taco Shredded Beef

1 boneless beef chuck roast (4 to 4½ pounds)
2 packages (1.0 ounce each) LAWRY'S® Taco Spices & Seasonings
1 medium onion, halved and sliced
2 teaspoons LAWRY'S® Seasoned Salt

Trim and discard all fat from meat; place meat in slow cooker. Sprinkle both packages of Taco Spices & Seasonings over meat and top with onion. Cover and cook on LOW for 8 to 10 hours. Remove beef to platter and shred with fork. Return meat to juices in slow cooker; stir in Seasoned Salt. Serve shredded meat in tacos, burritos, taquitos, flautas, on rolls or over cooked rice.

Makes 8 to 10 servings

Prep Time: 10 minutes
Slow Cooker Time: 8 to 10 hours

Chipotle Taco Filling

Beef Stew

5 potatoes, cut into chunks
5 carrots, cut into 1-inch pieces
3 pounds beef stew meat, cut into 1½-inch cubes
4 onions, quartered
2 stalks celery, chopped
1 can (about 28 ounces) diced tomatoes, undrained
1½ cups water
1 tablespoon plus 1½ teaspoons salt
1½ teaspoons paprika
1½ teaspoons Worcestershire sauce
¾ teaspoon black pepper
1 clove garlic, minced
1 bay leaf

1. Place potatoes, carrots, beef, onions, celery and tomatoes in 5-quart slow cooker. Combine water, salt, paprika, Worcestershire sauce, pepper, garlic and bay leaf in medium bowl; add to slow cooker.

2. Cover; cook on LOW 10 to 12 hours, stirring once.   *Makes 8 servings*

Helpful Hint

The stew meat available at supermarket meat counters is from less tender cuts of beef that are ideal for slow cooking. You can also purchase a chuck roast or boneless beef shoulder roast and cut it into cubes.

Beef Stew

Summer Squash Stew

2 pounds bulk Italian turkey sausage
4 cans (about 14 ounces each) diced tomatoes, undrained
5 medium yellow squash, thinly sliced
5 medium zucchini, thinly sliced
1 red onion, finely chopped
2 tablespoons dried Italian seasoning
1 tablespoon dried tomato, basil and garlic seasoning
4 cups (16 ounces) shredded Mexican cheese blend

1. Brown sausage 6 to 8 minutes in large nonstick skillet over medium-high heat, stirring to break up meat. Drain fat. Combine sausage, tomatoes, squash, zucchini, onion, Italian seasoning and garlic seasoning in 5-quart slow cooker; mix well.

2. Cover; cook on LOW 3 to 4 hours. Sprinkle cheese over stew. Cook, uncovered, 15 minutes or until cheese is melted. *Makes 6 servings*

Autumn Vegetables and Pork Chops

6 pork chops, ¾-inch thick
1 medium-size acorn squash
¾ cup packed brown sugar
3 tablespoons chopped green onion
2 tablespoons butter, melted
2 tablespoons orange juice
1 teaspoon Worcestershire sauce
1 teaspoon grated orange peel
¼ teaspoon ground cinnamon
⅛ teaspoon ground nutmeg
2 cups frozen green peas

Slice acorn squash in half, remove seeds and slice each half into 6 slices, approximately ½ inch thick. Place 6 half slices on bottom of 5-quart slow cooker. Arrange 3 pork chops over squash; repeat layers. Combine remaining ingredients except peas; pour over squash mixture. Cover and cook on LOW 5 to 6 hours or until pork and squash are tender. Remove both from slow cooker; keep warm. Stir in frozen peas. Turn heat setting to HIGH. Cover and cook about 5 minutes or until peas are tender; drain.

Makes 6 servings

*Favorite recipe from **National Pork Board***

Summer Squash Stew

Barbara's Pork Chop Dinner

> 1 tablespoon butter
> 1 tablespoon olive oil
> 6 pork loin chops
> 1 can (10¾ ounces) condensed cream of chicken soup, undiluted
> 1 can (4 ounces) mushrooms, drained and chopped
> ¼ cup Dijon mustard
> ¼ cup chicken broth
> 2 cloves garlic, minced
> ½ teaspoon salt
> ½ teaspoon dried basil
> ¼ teaspoon black pepper
> 6 red potatoes, cut into thin slices
> 1 onion, sliced
> Chopped fresh parsley

1. Heat butter and oil in large skillet. Brown pork chops on both sides.

2. Combine soup, mushrooms, mustard, broth, garlic, salt, basil and pepper in slow cooker. Add potatoes and onion; stir to coat. Place pork chops on top of potato mixture.

3. Cover; cook on LOW 8 to 10 hours or on HIGH 4 to 5 hours. Sprinkle with parsley just before serving. *Makes 6 servings*

Helpful Hint

Condensed soups are an easy way to create sauces for slow cooker recipes. They provide concentrated flavor and smooth sauces. Use undiluted condensed soups unless directed otherwise in the recipe.

Barbara's Pork Chop Dinner

Beef with Apples & Sweet Potatoes

 1 boneless beef chuck shoulder roast (2 pounds)
 1 can (40 ounces) sweet potatoes, drained
 2 small onions, sliced
 2 apples, cored and sliced
 ½ cup beef broth
 2 cloves garlic, minced
 1 teaspoon salt
 1 teaspoon dried thyme, divided
 ¾ teaspoon black pepper, divided
 2 tablespoons cold water
 1 tablespoon cornstarch
 ¼ teaspoon ground cinnamon

1. Trim fat from beef; cut into 2-inch pieces. Place beef, sweet potatoes, onions, apples, broth, garlic, salt, ½ teaspoon thyme and ½ teaspoon pepper in slow cooker.

2. Cover; cook on LOW 8 to 9 hours. Transfer beef, sweet potatoes and apples to platter; keep warm. Let liquid stand 5 minutes to allow fat to rise. Skim off fat.

3. Combine water, cornstarch, remaining ½ teaspoon thyme, ¼ teaspoon pepper and cinnamon in small bowl until smooth; stir into cooking liquid. Cook 15 minutes on HIGH. Serve sauce with beef, sweet potatoes and apples.   *Makes 6 servings*

Beef with Apples & Sweet Potatoes

Mushroom-Beef Stew

1 pound beef stew meat
1 can (10¾ ounces) condensed cream of mushroom soup, undiluted
2 cans (4 ounces each) sliced mushrooms, drained
1 package (about 1 ounce) dry onion soup mix
  Hot cooked noodles or rice

1. Combine beef, soup, mushrooms and soup mix in slow cooker.

2. Cover; cook on LOW 8 to 10 hours. Serve over noodles.   *Makes 4 servings*

Italian Sausage and Peppers

3 medium bell peppers, cut into chunks
1 small onion, cut into thin wedges
3 cloves garlic, minced
1 pound hot or mild Italian sausage links
1 cup marinara sauce
¼ cup red wine or port wine
1 tablespoon cornstarch
1 tablespoon water
  Hot cooked spaghetti
¼ cup grated Parmesan or Romano cheese

1. Coat slow cooker with cooking spray. Place bell peppers, onion and garlic in bottom of slow cooker. Arrange sausage over vegetables. Combine marinara sauce and wine; pour into slow cooker.

2. Cover; cook on LOW 8 to 9 hours or on HIGH 4 to 5 hours or until sausage is no longer pink in center and vegetables are tender.

3. Transfer sausage to serving platter; cover with foil to keep warm. Skim off and discard fat from liquid in slow cooker. Turn heat to HIGH.

4. Mix cornstarch and water in small bowl until smooth; stir into slow cooker. Cook 15 minutes or until sauce is thickened, stirring once. Serve sauce over spaghetti and sausage; top with cheese.   *Makes 4 servings*

Mushroom-Beef Stew

Pot Roast

1 tablespoon vegetable oil
1 beef chuck shoulder roast (3 to 4 pounds)
6 medium potatoes, halved
6 carrots, sliced
2 onions, quartered
2 stalks celery, sliced
1 can (about 14 ounces) diced tomatoes, undrained
Salt and black pepper
Dried oregano
Water
1½ to 2 tablespoons all-purpose flour

1. Heat oil in large skillet over medium-low heat. Add roast; brown on all sides. Transfer to slow cooker.

2. Add potatoes, carrots, onions, celery and tomatoes with juice. Season with salt, pepper and oregano. Add enough water to cover bottom of slow cooker by about ½ inch.

3. Cover; cook on LOW 8 to 10 hours. Remove roast to platter. Let stand 15 minutes.

4. Transfer juices to small saucepan; whisk in flour until smooth. Cook and stir over medium heat until thickened. Slice roast and serve with gravy.

Makes 6 to 8 servings

Pot Roast

Slow-Cooked Korean Beef Short Ribs

4 to 4½ pounds beef short ribs
¼ cup chopped green onions
¼ cup tamari or soy sauce
¼ cup beef broth or water
1 tablespoon brown sugar
2 teaspoons minced fresh ginger
2 teaspoons minced garlic
½ teaspoon black pepper
2 teaspoons dark sesame oil
   Hot cooked rice or linguini pasta
2 teaspoons sesame seeds, toasted*

*To toast sesame seeds, spread in large dry skillet. Shake skillet over medium-low heat about 3 minutes or until seeds begin to pop and turn golden.

1. Place ribs in 5-quart slow cooker. Combine green onions, tamari, broth, brown sugar, ginger, garlic and pepper in medium bowl; mix well and pour over ribs.

2. Cover; cook on LOW 7 to 8 hours or until ribs are fork tender. Remove ribs from cooking liquid. Cool slightly. Trim excess fat. Cut rib meat into bite-size pieces, discarding bones and fat.

3. Let cooking liquid stand 5 minutes to allow fat to rise. Skim off fat. Stir sesame oil into liquid. Return beef to slow cooker. Cover; cook 15 to 30 minutes or until heated through.

4. Serve with rice and garnish with sesame seeds.   *Makes 6 servings*

Prep Time: 10 to 15 minutes
Cook Time: 7 to 8 hours

Slow-Cooked Korean Beef Short Ribs

Sweet and Sour Spareribs

4 pounds pork spareribs
2 cups dry sherry or chicken broth
½ cup pineapple, mango or guava juice
⅓ cup chicken broth
2 tablespoons packed light brown sugar
2 tablespoons cider vinegar
2 tablespoons soy sauce
1 clove garlic, minced
½ teaspoon salt
¼ teaspoon black pepper
⅛ teaspoon red pepper flakes
¼ cup water
2 tablespoons cornstarch

1. Preheat oven to 400°F. Place ribs in foil-lined shallow roasting pan.

2. Bake 30 minutes, turning once. Remove from oven. Cut meat into 2-rib portions. Place ribs in 5-quart slow cooker. Add sherry, pineapple juice, broth, brown sugar, vinegar, soy sauce, garlic, salt, black pepper and red pepper flakes to slow cooker.

3. Cover; cook on LOW 6 hours. Transfer ribs to platter; keep warm. Let liquid in slow cooker stand 5 minutes to allow fat to rise. Skim off fat.

4. Blend water and cornstarch in small bowl until smooth. Stir mixture into slow cooker; mix well. Cook, uncovered, on HIGH 15 minutes or until slightly thickened.

Makes 4 servings

Helpful Hint

Long, slow cooking maximizes the heat from red pepper flakes. To lessen the heat, add pepper flakes during the last 30 minutes of cooking rather than at the beginning of the cooking process.

Sweet and Sour Spareribs

Veal Stew with Horseradish

1¼ **pounds veal, cut into 1-inch cubes**
2 **medium sweet potatoes, peeled and cut into 1-inch pieces**
1 **can (about 14 ounces) diced tomatoes, undrained**
1 **package (10 ounces) frozen corn, thawed**
1 **package (9 ounces) frozen lima beans, thawed**
1 **large onion, chopped**
1 **cup vegetable broth**
1 **tablespoon chili powder**
1 **tablespoon extra-hot prepared horseradish**
1 **tablespoon honey**

1. Place veal, sweet potatoes, tomatoes, corn, beans, onion, broth, chili powder, horseradish and honey in slow cooker; mix well.

2. Cover; cook on LOW 7 to 8 hours or until veal is tender.   *Makes 6 servings*

Best-Ever Barbecued Ribs

1 **teaspoon** *each* **salt, paprika and dried thyme**
¼ **teaspoon black pepper**
⅛ **teaspoon ground red pepper**
3 to 3½ **pounds well-trimmed pork baby back ribs, cut into**
    4-rib pieces
¼ **cup ketchup**
2 **tablespoons packed brown sugar**
1 **tablespoon Worcestershire sauce**
1 **tablespoon soy sauce**

1. Coat 4-quart slow cooker with cooking spray. Combine salt, paprika, thyme, black pepper and ground red pepper; rub onto meaty sides of ribs. Place ribs in slow cooker.

2. Cover; cook on LOW 7 to 8 hours or on HIGH 3 to 3½ hours or until ribs are tender but not falling off the bone.

3. Combine ketchup, brown sugar, Worcestershire sauce and soy sauce; mix well. Remove ribs from slow cooker; discard liquid. Coat ribs with sauce; return to slow cooker. Cook on HIGH 30 minutes or until ribs are glazed.   *Makes 6 servings*

Veal Stew with Horseradish

Italian-Style Sausage with Rice

1 pound mild Italian sausage links, cut into 1-inch pieces
1 can (about 15 ounces) pinto beans, rinsed and drained
1 cup pasta sauce
1 green bell pepper, cut into strips
1 small onion, halved and sliced
½ teaspoon salt
¼ teaspoon black pepper
   Hot cooked rice
   Chopped fresh basil (optional)

1. Brown sausage 6 to 8 minutes in large nonstick skillet over medium heat, stirring to break up meat. Drain fat.

2. Place sausage, beans, pasta sauce, bell pepper, onion, salt and black pepper into slow cooker. Cover; cook on LOW 4 to 6 hours.

3. Serve with rice. Garnish with basil.   *Makes 4 to 5 servings*

Iron Range Pot Roast

1 (3-pound) boneless pork shoulder (Boston Butt) roast
2 teaspoons Italian seasoning
1 teaspoon fennel seed, crushed
1 teaspoon salt
½ teaspoon celery seed
½ teaspoon ground black pepper
2 large potatoes, peeled and cut into ¾-inch slices
4 garlic cloves, peeled and sliced
¾ cup beef broth (or water)

Mix together seasonings and rub over all surfaces of pork roast. Brown roast in a little oil in large skillet over medium-high heat, turning often to brown evenly. Place potatoes and garlic in 3½ to 4-quart slow cooker; pour broth over and top with browned pork roast. Cover and cook on LOW for 8 to 9 hours, until pork is very tender. Slice pork to serve with vegetables and juices.   *Makes 6 to 8 servings*

*Favorite recipe from **National Pork Board***

Italian-Style Sausage with Rice

Harvest Ham Supper

6 carrots, cut into 2-inch pieces
3 sweet potatoes, quartered
1½ pounds boneless ham
1 cup maple syrup

1. Layer carrots, potatoes and ham in slow cooker. Pour syrup over ham and vegetables.

2. Cover; cook on LOW 6 to 8 hours or until vegetables are tender.

Makes 6 servings

Dijon Pork Roast with Cranberries

¼ teaspoon allspice
¼ teaspoon salt
¼ teaspoon ground black pepper
1 boneless pork loin roast (2 to 2½ pounds), trimmed of excess fat
2 tablespoons *French's*® Honey Dijon Mustard
2 tablespoons honey
2 teaspoons grated orange peel
1⅓ cups *French's*® French Fried Onions, divided
1 cup dried cranberries

1. Combine allspice, salt and pepper; sprinkle over roast. Place meat in slow cooker. Blend mustard, honey and orange peel; pour over roast. Sprinkle with ⅔ *cup* French Fried Onions and cranberries.

2. Cover and cook on LOW for 4 to 6 hours (or on HIGH for 2 to 3 hours) until meat is fork-tender.

3. Remove pork to serving platter. Skim fat from sauce in slow cooker; transfer sauce to serving bowl. Slice meat and serve with fruit sauce; sprinkle with remaining onions.

Makes 6 servings

Note: Cook times vary depending on type of slow cooker used. Check manufacturer's recommendations for cooking pork roast.

Prep Time: 10 minutes
Cook Time: 4 to 6 hours (LOW)

Harvest Ham Supper

Mexican Meatloaf

2 pounds ground beef
2 cups crushed corn chips
1 cup (4 ounces) shredded Cheddar cheese
⅔ cup salsa
2 eggs, beaten
¼ cup taco seasoning
½ cup ketchup
2 tablespoons brown sugar
1 teaspoon dry mustard

1. Combine beef, chips, cheese, salsa, eggs and taco seasoning in large bowl; mix well. Shape meat mixture into loaf; place in slow cooker.

2. Cover; cook on LOW 8 to 10 hours. Combine ketchup, brown sugar and mustard in small bowl. Spread over meatloaf. Cover; cook on HIGH 15 minutes.

Makes 4 to 6 servings

Beef Stew with Bacon and Sweet Potatoes

1 pound beef stew meat, cut into 1-inch chunks
1 can (about 14 ounces) beef broth
2 medium sweet potatoes, peeled, cut into 2-inch chunks
1 large onion, cut into 1½-inch chunks
2 slices thick-cut bacon, diced
1 teaspoon *each* salt and dried thyme
¼ teaspoon black pepper
2 tablespoons *each* cornstarch and water

1. Coat slow cooker with cooking spray. Combine beef, broth, sweet potatoes, onion, bacon, salt, thyme and pepper in slow cooker; mix well.

2. Cover; cook on LOW 7 to 8 hours or on HIGH 4 to 5 hours or until meat and vegetables are tender. Transfer beef and vegetables to serving bowl, using slotted spoon; cover with foil to keep warm.

3. Turn slow cooker to HIGH. Mix cornstarch with water in small bowl until smooth. Stir into juices; cover and cook 15 minutes or until thickened. Spoon sauce over beef and vegetables.

Makes 4 servings

Mexican Meatloaf

Slow Cooker Steak Fajitas

  1 beef flank steak (about 1 pound)
  1 medium onion, cut into strips
  ½ cup medium salsa, plus additional for serving
  2 tablespoons *each* chopped fresh cilantro and lime juice
  2 cloves garlic, minced
  1 tablespoon chili powder
  1 teaspoon ground cumin
  ½ teaspoon salt
  1 small green bell pepper, cut into strips
  1 small red bell pepper, cut into strips
   Flour tortillas, warmed

1. Cut flank steak lengthwise in half, then crosswise into thin strips. Combine onion, ½ cup salsa, cilantro, lime juice, garlic, chili powder, cumin and salt in slow cooker.

2. Cover; cook on LOW 5 to 6 hours. Add bell peppers. Cover; cook on LOW 1 hour. Serve with flour tortillas and additional salsa.   *Makes 4 servings*

Red Beans and Rice with Ham

  1 package (16 ounces) dried red beans, rinsed and sorted
  1 pound smoked beef sausage, sliced
  1 ham slice (about 8 ounces), cubed
  1 small onion, diced
 2½ to 3 cups water
  1 teaspoon Mexican (adobo) seasoning with pepper
  ⅛ teaspoon ground red pepper
   Hot cooked rice

1. Place beans in large bowl; cover completely with water. Soak 6 to 8 hours or overnight. Drain.

2. Place beans, sausage, ham, onion, water (2½ cups for LOW or 3 cups for HIGH), Mexican seasoning and red pepper in slow cooker.

3. Cover; cook on LOW 7 to 8 hours or on HIGH 3 to 4 hours or until beans are tender, stirring every 2 hours. Serve over rice.   *Makes 6 servings*

Slow Cooker Steak Fajitas

Potluck Poultry

Chicken with Italian Sausage

10 ounces bulk mild or hot Italian sausage
6 boneless skinless chicken thighs
1 can (about 15 ounces) cannellini or Great Northern beans, rinsed and drained
1 can (about 15 ounces) red beans, rinsed and drained
1 cup chicken broth
1 medium onion, chopped
1 teaspoon black pepper
½ teaspoon salt
Chopped fresh parsley (optional)

1. Brown sausage in large skillet over medium-high heat, stirring to break up meat. Drain fat. Spoon sausage into slow cooker.

2. Place chicken, beans, broth, onion, pepper and salt in slow cooker. Cover; cook on LOW 5 to 6 hours.

3. Slice each chicken thigh on the diagonal. Serve with sausage and beans. Garnish with parsley. *Makes 6 servings*

Prep Time: 15 minutes
Cook Time: 5 to 6 hours

Chicken with Italian Sausage

Chinese Cashew Chicken

1 pound fresh bean sprouts *or* 1 can (16 ounces) bean sprouts, drained
2 cups sliced cooked chicken
1 can (10¾ ounces) condensed cream of mushroom soup, undiluted
1 cup sliced celery
½ cup chopped green onions
1 can (4 ounces) sliced mushrooms, drained
3 tablespoons butter
1 tablespoon soy sauce
1 cup whole cashews
Hot cooked rice

1. Combine bean sprouts, chicken, soup, celery, green onions, mushrooms, butter and soy sauce in slow cooker; mix well.

2. Cover; cook on LOW 4 to 6 hours or on HIGH 2 to 3 hours. Stir in cashews just before serving. Serve with rice. *Makes 4 servings*

Italian Stew

1 can (about 14 ounces) chicken broth
1 can (about 14 ounces) Italian stewed tomatoes with peppers and onions, undrained
1 package (9 ounces) fully cooked spicy chicken sausage, sliced
2 carrots, thinly sliced
2 small zucchini, sliced
1 can (about 16 ounces) Great Northern, cannellini or navy beans, rinsed and drained
2 tablespoons chopped fresh basil (optional)

1. Coat slow cooker with cooking spray. Combine broth, tomatoes, sausage, carrots and zucchini in slow cooker. Cover; cook on LOW 6 to 7 hours or HIGH 3 to 4 hours or until vegetables are tender.

2. Turn slow cooker to HIGH; stir in beans. Cover; cook 10 to 15 minutes or until beans are heated through. Ladle into shallow bowls. Garnish with basil.
Makes 4 servings

Chinese Cashew Chicken

Turkey with Pecan-Cherry Stuffing

1 fresh or frozen boneless turkey breast (about 3 to 4 pounds), thawed if frozen
2 cups cooked rice
⅓ cup chopped pecans
⅓ cup dried cherries or cranberries
1 teaspoon poultry seasoning
¼ cup peach, apricot or plum preserves
1 teaspoon Worcestershire sauce

1. Remove and discard skin from turkey breast. Cut slices three-fourths of the way through turkey at 1-inch intervals.

2. Combine rice, pecans, cherries and poultry seasoning in large bowl; mix well. Stuff rice mixture between turkey slices. If needed, skewer turkey lengthwise to hold it together.

3. Place turkey in slow cooker. Cover; cook on LOW 5 to 6 hours or until turkey registers 170°F on meat thermometer inserted into thickest part of breast, not touching stuffing.

4. Stir preserves and Worcestershire sauce; spoon over turkey. Cover; let stand 5 minutes. Remove skewer before serving.   *Makes 8 servings*

Cheesy Slow Cooker Chicken

6 boneless skinless chicken breasts (about 1½ pounds)
Salt, black pepper and garlic powder
2 cans (10¾ ounces each) condensed cream of chicken soup, undiluted
1 can (10¾ ounces) condensed Cheddar cheese soup, undiluted
Chopped fresh parsley (optional)

1. Place 3 chicken breasts in slow cooker. Sprinkle with salt, pepper and garlic powder. Repeat with remaining 3 breasts and seasonings.

2. Combine soups in medium bowl; pour over chicken. Cover; cook on LOW 6 to 8 hours or until chicken is tender. Garnish with parsley.   *Makes 6 servings*

Turkey with Pecan-Cherry Stuffing

Chicken Sausage Pilaf

1 pound chicken or turkey sausage, casings removed
1 cup uncooked rice and pasta mix
4 cups chicken broth
2 stalks celery, diced
¼ cup slivered almonds
Salt and black pepper

1. Brown sausage in large nonstick skillet over medium heat, stirring to break up meat. Drain fat. Add rice and pasta mix to skillet. Cook 1 minute. Place mixture in slow cooker.

2. Add broth, celery, almonds, salt and pepper to slow cooker; mix well.

3. Cover; cook on LOW 7 to 10 hours or on HIGH 3 to 4 hours.

Makes 4 servings

Arroz con Pollo

6 chicken thighs, skin removed
1 can (14½ ounces) chicken broth
1 can (14½ ounces) stewed tomatoes
1 package (10 ounces) frozen peas
1 package (8 ounces) Spanish-style yellow rice mix
1½ cups *French's*® French Fried Onions, divided

1. Coat slow cooker with vegetable cooking spray. Combine chicken, broth and tomatoes in slow cooker. Cover and cook on LOW setting for 4 to 5 hours (or on HIGH for 2 to 2½ hours) until chicken is fork-tender.

2. Stir in peas and rice mix. Cover and cook on LOW setting for 2 to 3 hours (or on HIGH for 1 to 1½ hours) until rice is cooked and all liquid is absorbed. Stir in ¾ cup French Fried Onions. Spoon soup into serving bowls; top with remaining onions.

Makes 6 servings

Note: Cook times vary depending on type of slow cooker used. Check manufacturer's recommendations for cooking chicken and rice.

Prep Time: 10 minutes
Cook Time: 6 to 8 hours (LOW) or 3 to 4 hours (HIGH)

Chicken Sausage Pilaf

Easy Parmesan Chicken

8 ounces mushrooms, sliced*
1 medium onion, cut into thin wedges
1 tablespoon olive oil
4 boneless skinless chicken breasts
1 jar (26 ounces) pasta sauce
½ teaspoon dried basil
¼ teaspoon dried oregano
1 bay leaf
½ cup (2 ounces) shredded mozzarella cheese
¼ cup grated Parmesan cheese
Hot cooked spaghetti

*Or substitute sliced zucchini, cubed eggplant or broccoli florets.

1. Place mushrooms and onion in slow cooker.

2. Heat oil in large skillet over medium-high heat. Lightly brown chicken on both sides. Place chicken in slow cooker. Pour pasta sauce over chicken; add basil, oregano and bay leaf. Cover; cook on LOW 6 to 7 hours or on HIGH 3 to 4 hours or until chicken is tender. Remove and discard bay leaf.

3. Sprinkle chicken with cheeses. Cook, uncovered, on LOW 15 to 30 minutes or until cheeses are melted. Serve over spaghetti.   *Makes 4 servings*

Mile-High Enchilada Pie

8 (6-inch) corn tortillas
1 jar (12 ounces) prepared salsa
1 can (about 15 ounces) kidney beans, rinsed and drained
1 cup shredded cooked chicken
1 cup shredded Monterey Jack cheese with jalapeño peppers

1. Prepare foil handles for slow cooker (see page 15); place in slow cooker. Place 1 tortilla on bottom of slow cooker. Top with small amount of salsa, beans, chicken and cheese. Repeat layering with remaining ingredients, ending with tortilla and cheese.

2. Cover; cook on LOW 6 to 8 hours or on HIGH 3 to 4 hours. Lift out with foil handles.   *Makes 4 to 6 servings*

Easy Parmesan Chicken

Mu Shu Turkey

1 can (16 ounces) plums, drained and pitted
½ cup orange juice
¼ cup finely chopped onion
1 tablespoon minced fresh ginger
¼ teaspoon ground cinnamon
1 pound boneless turkey breast, cut into thin strips
6 (7-inch) flour tortillas
3 cups coleslaw mix

1. Place plums in blender or food processor; process until almost smooth. Combine plums, orange juice, onion, ginger and cinnamon in slow cooker; mix well. Place turkey over plum mixture.

2. Cover; cook on LOW 3 to 4 hours.

3. Divide turkey evenly among tortillas. Spoon about 2 tablespoons plum sauce over turkey; top with about ½ cup coleslaw mix. Fold bottom edge of tortilla over filling; fold in sides. Roll up to completely enclose filling. Repeat with remaining tortillas. Use remaining plum sauce for dipping. *Makes 6 servings*

Sweet Jalapeño Mustard Turkey Thighs

3 turkey thighs, skin removed
¾ cup honey mustard
½ cup orange juice
1 tablespoon cider vinegar
1 teaspoon Worcestershire sauce
1 to 2 fresh jalapeño peppers,* finely chopped
1 clove garlic, minced
½ teaspoon grated orange peel

*Jalapeño peppers can sting and irritate the skin; wear rubber gloves when handling peppers and do not touch eyes.

1. Place turkey in single layer in slow cooker. Combine mustard, orange juice, vinegar, Worcestershire sauce, jalapeños, garlic and orange peel in large bowl. Pour mixture over turkey.

2. Cover; cook on LOW 5 to 6 hours or until turkey is tender. *Makes 6 servings*

Mu Shu Turkey

French Country Slow Cooker Chicken

**1 medium onion, chopped
4 carrots, cut into ¼-inch slices
4 stalks celery, cut into slices
6 to 8 boneless skinless chicken breasts (about 1½ to 2 pounds)
1 teaspoon *each* dried tarragon and dried thyme
1 can (10¾ ounces) condensed cream of chicken soup, undiluted
1 envelope (about 1 ounce) dry onion soup mix
⅓ cup white wine or apple juice
2 tablespoons cornstarch**

1. Place onion, carrots and celery in slow cooker; top with chicken. Sprinkle with tarragon and thyme. Pour soup over chicken. Sprinkle with dry soup mix.

2. Cover; cook on HIGH 3 to 4 hours, stirring once.

3. Blend wine and cornstarch in small bowl until smooth. Stir into slow cooker. Cook, uncovered, 15 minutes or until sauce thickens.   *Makes 6 to 8 servings*

Tuscan Pasta

**1 pound boneless skinless chicken breasts, cut into 1-inch pieces
2 cans (about 14 ounces each) Italian-style stewed tomatoes
1 can (about 15 ounces) red kidney beans, rinsed and drained
1 can (about 15 ounces) tomato sauce
1 cup water
1 jar (4 ounces) sliced mushrooms, drained
1 medium green bell pepper, chopped
½ cup *each* chopped onion and chopped celery
4 cloves garlic, minced
1 teaspoon Italian seasoning
6 ounces uncooked thin spaghetti, broken in half**

1. Place chicken, stewed tomatoes, beans, tomato sauce, water, mushrooms, pepper, onion, celery, garlic and Italian seasoning in slow cooker.

2. Cover; cook on LOW 4 hours or until vegetables are tender.

3. Stir in spaghetti. Cook on HIGH 10 minutes; stir. Cover; cook 30 minutes or until spaghetti is tender.   *Makes 8 servings*

French Country Slow Cooker Chicken

South-of-the-Border Cumin Chicken

    3 bell peppers, thinly sliced
    1 small onion, chopped
    4 chicken drumsticks
    4 chicken thighs
    1 can (about 14 ounces) stewed tomatoes
    1 tablespoon mild green pepper sauce
    2 teaspoons sugar
1¾ teaspoons ground cumin, divided
1¼ teaspoons salt
    1 teaspoon dried oregano
¼ cup chopped fresh cilantro
    1 to 2 medium limes, cut into wedges
    Hot cooked rice

1. Place bell peppers and onion in slow cooker; arrange chicken on top. Combine tomatoes, pepper sauce, sugar, 1 teaspoon cumin, salt and oregano in large bowl. Pour over chicken mixture.

2. Cover; cook on LOW 8 hours or on HIGH 4 hours or until meat is just beginning to fall off bone.

3. Place chicken in shallow serving bowl. Stir remaining ¾ teaspoon cumin into tomato mixture and pour over chicken. Sprinkle with cilantro and serve with lime wedges. Serve over rice. *Makes 4 servings*

South-of-the-Border Cumin Chicken

Turkey Mushroom Stew

1 pound turkey cutlets, cut into 4×1-inch strips
1 small onion, thinly sliced
2 tablespoons minced green onion
8 ounces mushrooms, sliced
1 cup half-and-half or milk
2 to 3 tablespoons all-purpose flour
1 teaspoon salt
1 teaspoon dried tarragon
½ cup peas
½ cup sour cream
Puff pastry shells, baked

1. Layer turkey, onion, green onions and mushrooms in slow cooker. Cover; cook on LOW 4 hours.

2. Remove turkey and vegetables to serving bowl. Blend half-and-half, flour, salt and tarragon until smooth. Stir into slow cooker. Return cooked vegetables and turkey to slow cooker. Stir in peas.

3. Cover; cook on HIGH 30 to 45 minutes or until sauce is thickened and peas are heated through. Stir in sour cream just before serving. Serve in puff pastry shells.

Makes 4 servings

Turkey Mushroom Stew

Chicken Teriyaki

  1 **pound boneless skinless chicken tenders**
  1 **can (6 ounces) pineapple juice**
¼ **cup soy sauce**
  1 **tablespoon sugar**
  1 **tablespoon minced fresh ginger**
  1 **tablespoon minced garlic**
  1 **tablespoon vegetable oil**
  1 **tablespoon molasses**
 24 **cherry tomatoes (optional)**
  2 **cups hot cooked rice**

1. Combine chicken, pineapple juice, soy sauce, sugar, ginger, garlic, oil, molasses and tomatoes, if desired, in slow cooker.

2. Cover; cook on LOW 2 hours or until chicken is tender. Serve chicken and sauce over rice. *Makes 4 servings*

Continental Chicken

  1 **package (2¼ ounces) dried beef, cut into pieces**
  4 **boneless skinless chicken breasts (about 1 pound)**
  4 **slices bacon**
  1 **can (10¾ ounces) condensed cream of mushroom soup, undiluted**
¼ **cup all-purpose flour**
¼ **cup sour cream**
    Hot cooked noodles

1. Spray inside of slow cooker with nonstick cooking spray. Place dried beef in slow cooker. Wrap each piece of chicken with one bacon slice. Place wrapped chicken on top of dried beef. Combine soup and flour in medium bowl; mix until smooth. Pour over chicken.

2. Cover; cook on LOW 7 to 9 hours or on HIGH 3 to 4 hours. Add sour cream during last 30 minutes of cooking. Serve over noodles. *Makes 4 servings*

Chicken Teriyaki

Creamy Chicken

3 boneless skinless chicken breasts
2 cans (10¾ ounces each) condensed cream of chicken soup, undiluted
1 can (about 14 ounces) chicken broth
1 can (4 ounces) sliced mushrooms, drained
½ medium onion, diced
Salt and black pepper

1. Place chicken, soup, broth, mushrooms and onion in slow cooker.

2. Cover; cook on LOW 6 to 8 hours. Season with salt and pepper.

Makes 3 servings

Note: If desired, you may add cubed processed cheese spread before serving; cook on HIGH 10 minutes or until cheese is melted.

Chicken Parisienne

6 boneless skinless chicken breasts, cubed
½ teaspoon salt
½ teaspoon black pepper
½ teaspoon paprika
1 can (10¾ ounces) condensed cream of mushroom soup or cream of chicken soup, undiluted
2 cans (4 ounces each) sliced mushrooms, drained
½ cup dry white wine
1 cup sour cream
6 cups hot cooked egg noodles

1. Place chicken in slow cooker. Sprinkle with salt, pepper and paprika. Add soup, mushrooms and wine to slow cooker; mix well.

2. Cover; cook on HIGH 2 to 3 hours.

3. Add sour cream during last 30 minutes of cooking. Serve over noodles.

Makes 6 servings

Creamy Chicken

Chicken Stew

4 to 5 cups chopped cooked chicken (about 5 boneless skinless
    chicken breasts)
1 can (about 28 ounces) whole tomatoes, cut up, undrained
2 large potatoes, peeled and cut into 1-inch pieces
8 ounces fresh okra, sliced
1 large onion, chopped
1 can (14 ounces) cream-style corn
½ cup ketchup
½ cup barbecue sauce

1. Combine chicken, tomatoes, potatoes, okra and onion in slow cooker.

2. Cover; cook on LOW 6 to 8 hours or until potatoes are tender.

3. Add corn, ketchup and barbecue sauce. Cover; cook on HIGH 30 minutes.

Makes 6 servings

Southwestern-Style Chicken

1 package (about 1¼ ounces) taco seasoning mix
¼ cup all-purpose flour
6 to 8 boneless skinless chicken thighs *or* 4 boneless skinless
    breasts, cut into halves
2 tablespoons vegetable oil
1 large onion, cut into 1-inch pieces
2 green bell peppers, cut into 1-inch pieces
1 can (about 14 ounces) diced tomatoes with jalapeños, undrained
    Salt and pepper

1. Reserve 1 teaspoon taco seasoning. Combine flour and remaining seasoning in
large resealable food storage bag. Add chicken, 1 to 2 pieces at a time; shake to
coat.

2. Heat oil in large skillet over medium-high heat; brown chicken. Transfer chicken to
slow cooker; sprinkle with reserved 1 teaspoon seasoning. Add onion to skillet; cook
and stir until translucent. Place onion, bell peppers and tomatoes in slow cooker.

3. Cover; cook on LOW 6 to 7 hours or until chicken is tender. Season with salt and
pepper.

Makes 4 to 6 servings

Chicken Stew

Nice 'n' Easy Italian Chicken

4 boneless skinless chicken breasts
1 jar (26 ounces) pasta sauce
8 ounces mushrooms, sliced
1 medium green bell pepper, chopped
1 medium zucchini, diced
1 medium onion, chopped
Hot cooked pasta

1. Combine chicken, pasta sauce, mushrooms, bell pepper, zucchini and onion in slow cooker.

2. Cover; cook on LOW 6 to 8 hours or until chicken is tender. Serve over pasta.

Makes 4 servings

Sweet Chicken Curry

1 pound boneless skinless chicken breasts, cut into 1-inch pieces
1 large green or red bell pepper, cut into 1-inch pieces
1 large onion, sliced
1 large tomato, seeded and chopped
½ cup prepared mango chutney
¼ cup water
2 tablespoons cornstarch
1½ teaspoons curry powder
Hot cooked rice

1. Place chicken, bell pepper and onion in slow cooker; top with tomato. Mix chutney, water, cornstarch and curry powder in small bowl; pour over chicken.

2. Cover; cook on LOW 3½ to 4½ hours or until chicken is tender. Serve over rice.

Makes 4 servings

Nice 'n' Easy Italian Chicken

Coq au Vin

2 cups frozen pearl onions, thawed
4 slices thick-cut bacon, crisp-cooked and crumbled
1 cup sliced button mushrooms
1 clove garlic, minced
1 teaspoon dried thyme
⅛ teaspoon black pepper
6 boneless skinless chicken breasts (about 2 pounds)
½ cup dry red wine
¾ cup chicken broth
¼ cup tomato paste
3 tablespoons all-purpose flour
Hot cooked egg noodles

1. Layer onions, bacon, mushrooms, garlic, thyme, pepper, chicken, wine and broth in slow cooker.

2. Cover; cook on LOW 6 to 8 hours.

3. Remove chicken and vegetables; cover and keep warm. Ladle ½ cup cooking liquid into small bowl; cool slightly. Mix reserved liquid, tomato paste and flour until smooth; stir into slow cooker. Cook; uncovered, on HIGH 15 minutes or until thickened. Serve over hot noodles. *Makes 6 servings*

Helpful Hint

The flavor of wine intensifies with long cooking, so use a good inexpensive wine that you would find drinkable.

Coq au Vin

Southwest Turkey Tenderloin Stew

1½ pounds turkey tenderloin, cut into ¾-inch pieces
1 tablespoon chili powder
1 teaspoon ground cumin
¼ teaspoon salt
1 can (about 15 ounces) chili beans in spicy sauce, undrained
1 can (about 14 ounces) chili-style stewed tomatoes, undrained
¾ cup prepared salsa or picante sauce
1 red bell pepper, cut into ¾-inch pieces
1 green bell pepper, cut into ¾-inch pieces
¾ cup chopped red or yellow onion
3 cloves garlic, minced
Fresh cilantro (optional)

1. Place turkey in slow cooker. Sprinkle with chili powder, cumin and salt; toss to coat. Add beans, tomatoes, salsa, bell peppers, onion and garlic; mix well.

2. Cover; cook on LOW 5 to 6 hours. Ladle into bowls. Garnish with cilantro.

Makes 6 servings

Helpful Hint

To tame the spiciness of this recipe, you can substitute chili beans in mild sauce for the spicy version. Be sure to chose a mild salsa.

Southwest Turkey Tenderloin Stew

Chicken Pilaf

2 pounds chopped cooked chicken
2 cans (8 ounces each) tomato sauce
2½ cups water
1⅓ cups uncooked converted long-grain rice
1 cup chopped onion
1 cup chopped celery
1 cup chopped green bell pepper
⅔ cup sliced black olives
¼ cup sliced almonds
¼ cup (½ stick) butter or margarine
2 cloves garlic, minced
2½ teaspoons salt
½ teaspoon ground allspice
½ teaspoon ground turmeric
¼ teaspoon curry powder
¼ teaspoon black pepper

1. Combine chicken, tomato sauce, water, rice, onion, celery, bell pepper, olives, almonds, butter, garlic, salt, allspice, turmeric, curry powder and black pepper in slow cooker; stir well.

2. Cover; cook on LOW 6 to 8 hours or on HIGH 3 to 4 hours.

Makes 10 servings

Helpful Hint

Rice has a tendency to become mushy when cooked for many hours in a slow cooker. For best results, choose uncooked, converted long-grain rice and begin checking for doneness during the last 30 minutes of cooking.

Chicken Pilaf

Super-Easy Sandwiches

Easy Homemade Barbecue Sandwiches

1 boneless pork shoulder roast (3 to 4 pounds)
Salt and black pepper
1 bottle (16 ounces) barbecue sauce
Hamburger buns or sandwich rolls

1. Cover bottom of slow cooker with ½-inch water. Place roast in slow cooker; season with salt and pepper.

2. Cover; cook on LOW 8 to 10 hours.

3. Remove roast from slow cooker; let stand 15 minutes. Discard cooking liquid. Shred roast using two forks. Return to slow cooker. Add barbecue sauce; mix well. Cover and cook on HIGH 30 minutes.

4. Meanwhile, toast hamburger buns. Serve mixture on buns.

Makes 8 to 10 servings

Serving Suggestion: Serve with your favorite coleslaw recipe.

Easy Homemade Barbecue Sandwich

Hot & Juicy Reuben Sandwiches

        1 mild-cure corned beef (about 1½ pounds)
        2 cups sauerkraut, drained
        ½ cup beef broth
        1 small onion, sliced
        1 clove garlic, minced
        ¼ teaspoon caraway seeds
        4 to 6 peppercorns
        8 slices pumpernickel or rye bread
        4 slices Swiss cheese
          Mustard

1. Trim excess fat from corned beef. Place in slow cooker. Add sauerkraut, broth, onion, garlic, caraway seeds and peppercorns.

2. Cover; cook on LOW 7 to 9 hours.

3. Remove beef from slow cooker. Cut against the grain into ¼-inch-thick slices. Divide evenly on 4 slices bread. Top each with ½ cup drained sauerkraut mixture and one slice cheese. Spread mustard on remaining 4 bread slices. Close sandwiches.

Makes 4 servings

Note: This two-fisted stack of corned beef, sauerkraut and Swiss cheese makes a glorious sandwich you'll serve often.

Prep Time: 25 minutes
Cook Time: 7 to 9 hours

Hot & Juicy Reuben Sandwich

Best Beef Brisket Sandwich Ever

1 beef brisket (about 3 pounds)
2 cups apple cider, divided
⅓ cup chopped fresh thyme *or* 2 tablespoons dried thyme
1 head garlic, cloves separated, peeled and crushed
2 tablespoons whole peppercorns
1 tablespoon mustard seeds
1 tablespoon Cajun seasoning
1 teaspoon ground cumin
1 teaspoon celery seeds
1 teaspoon ground allspice
2 to 4 whole cloves
1 bottle (12 ounces) dark beer
10 to 12 sourdough sandwich rolls, halved

1. Place brisket, ½ cup cider, thyme, garlic, peppercorns, mustard seeds, Cajun seasoning, cumin, celery seeds, allspice and cloves in large resealable food storage bag. Seal bag; marinate in refrigerator overnight.

2. Place brisket and marinade in slow cooker. Add remaining 1½ cups apple cider and beer.

3. Cover; cook on LOW 10 hours or until brisket is tender. Strain sauce. Slice brisket; combine with sauce. Serve on rolls.   *Makes 10 to 12 servings*

Serving Suggestion: For extra-special flavor, serve these sandwiches with mustard spread or horseradish sauce.

Best Beef Brisket Sandwich Ever

Barbecued Beef Sandwiches

3 pounds boneless beef chuck shoulder roast
2 cups ketchup
1 medium onion, chopped
¼ cup cider vinegar
¼ cup dark molasses
2 tablespoons Worcestershire sauce
2 cloves garlic, minced
½ teaspoon salt
½ teaspoon dry mustard
½ teaspoon black pepper
¼ teaspoon garlic powder
¼ teaspoon red pepper flakes
Sesame seed buns, split

1. Cut roast in half; place in slow cooker. Combine ketchup, onion, vinegar, molasses, Worcestershire sauce, garlic, salt, dry mustard, black pepper, garlic powder and red pepper flakes in large bowl. Pour sauce mixture over roast.

2. Cover; cook on LOW 8 to 10 hours or on HIGH 4 to 5 hours. Remove roast from sauce; cool slightly. Trim and discard excess fat. Shred meat using two forks. Let sauce stand 5 minutes to allow fat to rise. Skim off fat.

3. Return shredded beef to slow cooker; stir evenly to coat with sauce. Adjust seasonings. Cover; cook 15 to 30 minutes or until heated through.

4. Spoon filling onto buns and top with additional sauce, if desired.

Makes 12 servings

Barbecued Beef Sandwich

Slow-Cooked Kielbasa in a Bun

1 pound kielbasa, cut into 4 (4- to 5-inch) pieces
1 large onion, thinly sliced
1 large green bell pepper, cut into strips
¼ teaspoon salt
¼ teaspoon dried thyme
¼ teaspoon black pepper
½ cup chicken broth
4 hoagie rolls, split

1. Brown kielbasa in nonstick skillet over medium-high heat 3 to 4 minutes. Place in slow cooker. Add onion, bell pepper, salt, thyme and black pepper. Stir in broth.

2. Cover; cook on LOW 7 to 8 hours. Place kielbasa in rolls. Top with onion and bell pepper.   *Makes 4 servings*

Tip: For zesty flavor, top sandwiches with pickled peppers and a dollop of mustard.

Easy Beef Sandwiches

1 large onion, sliced
1 boneless beef bottom round roast (about 3 to 5 pounds)
1 cup water
1 package (1 ounce) au jus gravy mix
6 to 8 French bread rolls, split

1. Place onion in slow cooker; top with roast. Combine water and gravy mix in small bowl; pour over roast.

2. Cover and cook on LOW 7 to 9 hours or until beef is tender.

3. Transfer beef to cutting board. Shred beef using two forks; return beef to slow cooker. Cook on HIGH 10 minutes. Serve beef on rolls with juice on the side for dipping.   *Makes 6 to 8 servings*

Serving Suggestion: Add slices of provolone cheese to these sandwiches.

Slow-Cooked Kielbasa in a Bun

Italian Beef

1 beef rump roast (3 to 5 pounds)
1 can (about 14 ounces) beef broth
2 cups mild giardiniera
8 Italian bread rolls

1. Place rump roast in slow cooker; add broth and giardiniera.

2. Cover; cook on LOW 10 hours.

3. Transfer beef to cutting board. Shred beef using two forks; return to slow cooker. Cook on HIGH 10 minutes. Serve beef with sauce on rolls.   *Makes 8 servings*

Tex-Mex Beef Wraps

1 tablespoon chili powder
2 teaspoons ground cumin
1 teaspoon salt
¼ teaspoon ground red pepper
1 boneless beef chuck pot roast (2½ to 3 pounds), cut into 4 pieces
1 medium onion, chopped
3 cloves garlic, minced
1 cup salsa, divided
12 (6- to 7-inch) flour or corn tortillas, warmed
1 cup (4 ounces) shredded Cheddar or Monterey Jack cheese
1 cup chopped tomato
¼ cup chopped cilantro
1 ripe avocado, diced

1. Coat slow cooker with cooking spray. Blend chili powder, cumin, salt and red pepper in small bowl. Rub beef with spice mixture. Place onion and garlic in slow cooker; top with beef. Spoon ½ cup salsa over beef.

2. Cover; cook on LOW 8 to 9 hours or on HIGH 3½ to 4½ hours or until meat is very tender.

3. Transfer beef to cutting board. Shred beef using two forks. Skim off and discard fat from juices in slow cooker. Return beef to slow cooker; mix well. Place beef on warm tortillas; top with cheese, tomato, cilantro and avocado. Fold to enclose filling. Serve with remaining salsa.   *Makes 6 servings*

Italian Beef

BBQ Pork Sandwiches

4 pounds boneless pork loin roast, fat trimmed
1 can (14½ ounces) beef broth
⅓ cup _French's_® Worcestershire Sauce
⅓ cup _Frank's_® _RedHot_® Original Cayenne Pepper Sauce

Sauce
½ cup ketchup
½ cup molasses
¼ cup _French's_® Classic Yellow® Mustard
¼ cup _French's_® Worcestershire Sauce
2 tablespoons _Frank's_® _RedHot_® Original Cayenne Pepper Sauce

1. Place roast on bottom of slow cooker. Combine broth, _⅓ cup each_ Worcestershire and **_Frank's RedHot_** Sauce. Pour over roast. Cover and cook on HIGH 5 hours* or until roast is tender.

2. Meanwhile, combine ingredients for sauce in large bowl; set aside.

3. Transfer roast to large cutting board. Discard liquid. Coarsely chop roast. Stir into reserved sauce. Spoon pork mixture on large rolls. Serve with deli potato salad, if desired.   _Makes 8 to 10 servings_

*_Or cook 10 hours on LOW._

Tip: Make additional sauce and serve on the side. Great also with barbecued ribs and chops!

Prep Time: 10 minutes
Cook Time: 5 hours

BBQ Pork Sandwich

Suzie's Sloppy Joes

3 pounds ground beef
1 cup chopped onion
3 cloves garlic, minced
1¼ cups ketchup
1 cup chopped red bell pepper
5 tablespoons Worcestershire sauce
4 tablespoons brown sugar
3 tablespoons prepared mustard
3 tablespoons vinegar
2 teaspoons chili powder
Toasted hamburger buns

1. Brown ground beef, onion and garlic in large nonstick skillet over medium-high heat in two batches, stirring to break up meat. Drain fat.

2. Combine ketchup, bell pepper, Worcestershire sauce, brown sugar, mustard, vinegar and chili powder in slow cooker. Stir in beef mixture.

3. Cover; cook on LOW 6 to 8 hours. Spoon onto hamburger buns.

Makes 8 servings

Helpful Hint

To drain cooked ground meat, place it in a colander. Stir the meat briefly or shake the colander. You can also transfer the meat to the slow cooker using a slotted spoon, which will allow the fat to drain off as well.

Suzie's Sloppy Joes

Meatball Grinders

1 can (about 15 ounces) diced tomatoes, drained and juices reserved
1 can (8 ounces) tomato sauce
¼ cup chopped onion
2 tablespoons tomato paste
1 teaspoon dried Italian seasoning
1 pound ground chicken
½ cup fresh bread crumbs (1 slice bread)
1 egg white, lightly beaten
3 tablespoons finely chopped fresh parsley
2 cloves garlic, minced
¼ teaspoon salt
⅛ teaspoon black pepper
Nonstick cooking spray
4 small hard rolls, split
2 tablespoons grated Parmesan cheese

1. Combine diced tomatoes, ½ cup reserved juice, tomato sauce, onion, tomato paste and Italian seasoning in slow cooker. Cover; cook on LOW 3 to 4 hours or until onions are soft.

2. Halfway through cooking time, prepare meatballs. Combine chicken, bread crumbs, egg white, parsley, garlic, salt and pepper in medium bowl. Shape mixture into 12 to 16 meatballs.

3. Spray medium nonstick skillet with cooking spray; heat over medium heat. Add meatballs; cook about 8 to 10 minutes or until well browned on all sides.

4. Remove meatballs to slow cooker. Cook, covered, on LOW 1 to 2 hours or until meatballs are no longer pink in centers. Place 3 to 4 meatballs on each roll. Spoon sauce over meatballs. Sprinkle with cheese. *Makes 4 servings*

Meatball Grinder

Easy Beefy Sandwiches

1 boneless beef rump roast (2 to 4 pounds)
1 package (1 ounce) Italian salad dressing mix
1 package (1 ounce) dry onion soup mix
2 cubes beef bouillon
2 tablespoons prepared yellow mustard
1 cup water
   Salt, onion powder, garlic powder and black pepper
6 to 8 crusty rolls, split
   Provolone or mozzarella cheese slices

1. Place roast, salad dressing mix, soup mix, bouillon cubes and mustard in slow cooker. Add water.

2. Cover; cook on LOW 8 to 10 hours or until beef is tender. Season with salt, onion powder, garlic powder and pepper. Serve beef on rolls with cheese slices.

Makes 6 to 8 servings

Shredded Beef Fajitas

1 beef flank steak (about 1½ pounds), cut into 6 equal portions
1 can (about 14 ounces) diced tomatoes with jalapeños, undrained
1 cup chopped onion
1 medium green bell pepper, cut into ½-inch pieces
2 cloves garlic, minced *or* ¼ teaspoon garlic powder
1 package (1½ ounces) fajita seasoning mix
12 (8-inch) flour tortillas
   Toppings: sour cream, guacamole, shredded Cheddar cheese and salsa

1. Place steak in slow cooker. Add tomatoes, onion, bell pepper, garlic and seasoning mix to slow cooker.

2. Cover; cook on LOW 8 to 10 hours or on HIGH 4 to 5 hours or until beef is tender. Transfer beef to cutting board. Shred beef using two forks; return to slow cooker. Cook on HIGH 10 minutes.

3. To serve, divide beef mixture evenly into flour tortillas. Add toppings as desired; roll up tortillas.

Makes 12 servings

Easy Beefy Sandwich

Hot Beef Sandwiches

1 chuck beef roast (3 to 4 pounds), cut into chunks
1 small jar (6 ounces) sliced dill pickles, undrained
1 medium onion, diced
1 teaspoon mustard seeds
4 cloves garlic, minced
1 can (about 14 ounces) crushed tomatoes with Italian seasoning
Hamburger buns
Toppings: lettuce, sliced tomatoes, red onion and pickles

1. Place beef in slow cooker. Pour pickles with juice over beef. Add onion, mustard seeds, garlic and tomatoes.

2. Cover; cook on LOW 8 to 10 hours.

3. Transfer beef to cutting board. Shred beef using two forks. Return to slow cooker; mix well. Serve beef mixture on toasted buns with desired toppings.

Makes 6 to 8 servings

BBQ Beef Sandwiches

1 boneless beef chuck roast (about 3 pounds)
¼ cup ketchup
2 tablespoons brown sugar
2 tablespoons red wine vinegar
1 tablespoon Dijon mustard
1 tablespoon Worcestershire sauce
1 clove garlic, crushed
¼ teaspoon salt
¼ teaspoon liquid smoke
⅛ teaspoon black pepper
10 to 12 French rolls or sandwich buns

1. Place beef in slow cooker. Mix ketchup, sugar, vinegar, mustard, Worcestershire sauce, garlic, salt, liquid smoke and pepper in medium bowl; pour over beef.

2. Cover; cook on LOW 8 to 9 hours.

3. Transfer beef to cutting board. Shred beef using two forks. Return beef to slower cooker; mix well. Serve beef on warmed rolls. *Makes 10 to 12 servings*

Hot Beef Sandwich

Easy Family Burritos

1 boneless beef chuck shoulder roast (2 to 3 pounds)
1 jar (24 ounces) *or* 2 jars (16 ounces each) salsa
   Flour tortillas
   Toppings: shredded cheese, sour cream, chopped lettuce, chopped tomato, chopped onion and guacamole

1. Place roast in slow cooker; top with salsa.

2. Cover; cook on LOW 8 to 10 hours.

3. Transfer beef to cutting board. Shred beef using two forks. Return to slow cooker; mix well. Cover; cook 1 to 2 hours or until heated through. Serve beef in warm tortillas with desired toppings. *Makes 8 servings*

Italian-Style Shredded Beef

1 (2½-pound) boneless eye of round beef roast
1 medium onion, thinly sliced
1 (6-ounce) can Italian flavored tomato paste
6 teaspoons HERB-OX® beef flavored bouillon
½ cup water
12 Kaiser rolls
12 (1-ounce) slices Provolone cheese

Place roast in a 3½-quart slow cooker. Add onion and remaining ingredients. Cover and cook on HIGH for 5 to 6 hours or until meat is tender. Remove roast from cooker. Using two forks, shred meat. Return meat to cooker; stirring to coat with sauce. Evenly divide meat among Kaiser rolls. Top with cheese and serve. *Makes 12 servings*

Prep Time: 10 minutes
Total Time: 6 hours, 10 minutes

Easy Family Burritos

Sloppy Sloppy Joes

4 pounds ground beef
1 cup chopped onion
1 cup chopped green bell pepper
1 can (about 28 ounces) tomato sauce
2 cans (10¾ ounces each) condensed tomato soup, undiluted
1 cup packed brown sugar
¼ cup ketchup
3 tablespoons Worcestershire sauce
1 tablespoon dry mustard
1 tablespoon prepared mustard
1½ teaspoons chili powder
1 teaspoon garlic powder
Hamburger buns

1. Brown beef 6 to 8 minutes in large skillet over medium-high heat, stirring to break up meat. Drain fat. Add onion and bell pepper; cook and stir 5 to 6 minutes over medium heat or until onion is translucent.

2. Transfer meat mixture to 4- or 5-quart slow cooker. Add tomato sauce, soup, brown sugar, ketchup, Worcestershire sauce, dry mustard, prepared mustard, chili powder and garlic powder; stir until well blended.

3. Cover; cook on LOW 4 to 6 hours. Serve on toasted buns.

Makes 20 to 25 servings

Sloppy Sloppy Joe

Piping Hot Soups

Simmering Hot & Sour Soup

  2 cans (about 14 ounces each) chicken broth
  1 cup chopped cooked chicken or pork
  4 ounces fresh shiitake mushroom caps, thinly sliced
  ½ cup sliced bamboo shoots, cut into thin strips
  3 tablespoons rice vinegar or rice wine vinegar
  2 tablespoons soy sauce
1½ teaspoons chili paste *or* 1 teaspoon hot chili oil
  4 ounces firm tofu, well drained and cut into ½-inch pieces
  2 teaspoons dark sesame oil
  2 tablespoons cornstarch
  2 tablespoons cold water
  Chopped cilantro

1. Combine broth, chicken, mushrooms, bamboo shoots, vinegar, soy sauce and chili paste in slow cooker. Cover; cook on LOW 3 to 4 hours.

2. Stir in tofu and sesame oil. Blend cornstarch and water until smooth. Stir into slow cooker. Cover; cook on HIGH 15 minutes or until soup is thickened.

3. Garnish with cilantro.   *Makes 4 servings*

Simmering Hot & Sour Soup

Italian Beef and Barley Soup

> **1 boneless beef top sirloin steak (about 1½ pounds)**
> **1 tablespoon vegetable oil**
> **4 medium carrots or parsnips, cut into ¼-inch slices**
> **1 cup chopped onion**
> **1 teaspoon dried thyme**
> **½ teaspoon dried rosemary**
> **¼ teaspoon black pepper**
> **⅓ cup pearl barley**
> **2 cans (about 14 ounces each) beef broth**
> **1 can (about 14 ounces) diced tomatoes with Italian seasoning, undrained**

1. Cut beef into 1-inch pieces. Heat oil over medium-high heat in large skillet. Brown beef on all sides.

2. Place carrots and onion in slow cooker; sprinkle with thyme, rosemary and pepper. Top with barley and beef. Pour broth and tomatoes over beef.

3. Cover; cook on LOW 8 to 10 hours.   *Makes 6 servings*

Prep Time: 20 minutes
Cook Time: 8 to 10 hours

Helpful Hint

Choose pearl barley rather than quick-cooking barley, which will become mushy during long cooking.

Italian Beef and Barley Soup

Nancy's Chicken Noodle Soup

    1 can (48 ounces) chicken broth
    2 boneless skinless chicken breasts, cut into bite-size pieces
    4 cups water
    ⅔ cup diced onion
    ⅔ cup diced celery
    ⅔ cup diced carrots
    ⅔ cup sliced mushrooms
    ½ cup frozen peas
    4 chicken bouillon cubes
    2 tablespoons margarine
    1 tablespoon parsley
    1 teaspoon salt
    1 teaspoon ground cumin
    1 teaspoon dried marjoram
    1 teaspoon black pepper
    2 cups cooked egg noodles

1. Combine broth, chicken, water, onion, celery, carrots, mushrooms, peas, bouillon, margarine, parsley, salt, cumin, marjoram and pepper in 5-quart slow cooker.

2. Cover; cook on LOW 5 to 7 hours or on HIGH 3 to 4 hours. Add noodles 30 minutes before serving. *Makes 4 servings*

Navy Bean & Ham Soup

    6 cups water
    5 cups dried navy beans, soaked overnight and drained
    1 pound ham, cubed
    1 can (15 ounces) corn, drained
    1 can (4 ounces) mild diced green chiles, drained
    Salt and black pepper

1. Combine water, beans, ham, corn, chiles, salt and pepper in slow cooker.

2. Cover; cook on LOW 8 to 10 hours or until beans are softened.
Makes 4 servings

Nancy's Chicken Noodle Soup

Clam Chowder

5 cans (10¾ ounces each) condensed cream of potato soup, undiluted
2 cans (12 ounces each) evaporated milk
2 cans (10 ounces each) whole baby clams, rinsed and drained
1 can (about 15 ounces) cream-style corn
2 cans (4 ounces each) tiny shrimp, rinsed and drained
¾ cup crisp-cooked and crumbled bacon (about ½ pound)
   Lemon pepper
   Oyster crackers

1. Combine soup, evaporated milk, clams, corn, shrimp, bacon and lemon pepper in 4-quart slow cooker.

2. Cover; cook on LOW 3 to 4 hours, stirring occasionally. Serve with oyster crackers.   *Makes 10 servings*

Beef, Barley & Onion Soup

2 pounds beef stew meat, (½-inch cubes)
3 large carrots, cut into ½-inch-thick slices
2 large ribs celery, cut into ½-inch-thick slices
4 cans (14½ ounces each) beef broth
½ teaspoon dried oregano leaves
½ teaspoon salt
¼ teaspoon ground black pepper
½ cup barley
2 cups *French's*® French Fried Onions, divided

1. Combine beef, carrots, celery, broth and seasonings in slow cooker. Cover; cook on LOW for 7 hours (or on HIGH for 3½ hours) until meat and vegetables are tender.

2. Stir in barley. Cover and cook on LOW for 1 hour (or on HIGH for ½ hour) until barley is tender. Stir in *1 cup* French Fried Onions. Spoon soup into serving bowls; sprinkle with remaining onions.   *Makes 8 servings*

Note: Cook times vary depending on type of slow cooker used. Check manufacturer's recommendations for cooking beef and barley.

Prep Time: 20 minutes
Cook Time: 8 hours

Clam Chowder

No-Chop Black Bean Soup

3 cans (about 15 ounces each) black beans, rinsed and drained
1 package (12 ounces) frozen diced green bell peppers, thawed
2 cups frozen chopped onion, thawed
2 cans (about 14 ounces each) chicken broth
1 can (about 14 ounces) diced tomatoes with pepper, celery and
    onion, undrained
1½ teaspoons ground cumin, divided
1 teaspoon minced garlic
2 tablespoons olive oil
¾ teaspoon salt

1. Combine beans, bell peppers, onions, broth, tomatoes, 1 teaspoon cumin and garlic in slow cooker.

2. Cover; cook on LOW 8 to 10 hours or on HIGH 4 to 5 hours. Stir in oil, salt and remaining ½ teaspoon cumin just before serving. *Makes 8 servings*

Butternut Squash-Apple Soup

3 packages (12 ounces each) frozen cooked winter squash, thawed
    and drained *or* about 4½ cups mashed cooked butternut squash
2 cans (about 14 ounces each) chicken broth*
1 medium Golden Delicious apple, peeled, cored and chopped
2 tablespoons minced onion
1 tablespoon packed light brown sugar
1 teaspoon minced fresh sage *or* ½ teaspoon ground sage
¼ teaspoon ground ginger
½ cup whipping cream or half-and-half

*For thicker soup, use only 3 cups chicken broth.

1. Combine squash, broth, apple, onion, brown sugar, sage and ginger in slow cooker.

2. Cover; cook on LOW about 6 hours or on HIGH about 3 hours.

3. Pour soup into food processor or blender; process until smooth. Stir in cream just before serving. *Makes 6 to 8 servings*

No-Chop Black Bean Soup

Beef Fajita Soup

1 pound beef stew meat
1 can (about 15 ounces) pinto beans, rinsed and drained
1 can (about 15 ounces) black beans, rinsed and drained
1 can (about 14 ounces) diced tomatoes with roasted garlic, undrained
1 can (about 14 ounces) beef broth
1 small green bell pepper, thinly sliced
1 small red bell pepper, thinly sliced
1 small onion, thinly sliced
1½ cups water
2 teaspoons ground cumin
1 teaspoon seasoned salt
1 teaspoon black pepper
Toppings: sour cream, shredded Monterey Jack or Cheddar cheese and chopped olives

1. Combine beef, beans, tomatoes, broth, bell peppers, onion, water, cumin, salt and black pepper in slow cooker.

2. Cover; cook on LOW 8 hours. Serve with desired toppings.

Makes 8 servings

Helpful Hint

Diced tomatoes with seasonings are a great time-saver when assembling ingredients for a slow cooker dish. Look for varieties with Italian seasoning, roasted garlic, mushrooms and garlic, and mild green chiles.

Beef Fajita Soup

Creamy Turkey Soup

2 cans (10¾ ounces each) condensed cream of chicken soup,
    undiluted
2 cups chopped cooked turkey breast
1 package (8 ounces) sliced mushrooms
1 medium yellow onion, chopped
1 teaspoon rubbed sage *or* ½ teaspoon dried poultry seasoning
1 cup frozen peas, thawed
½ cup milk
1 jar (about 4 ounces) diced pimiento

1. Combine soup, turkey, mushrooms, onion and sage in slow cooker.

2. Cover; cook on LOW 8 hours or on HIGH 4 hours.

3. Stir in peas, milk and pimiento. Cover; cook on HIGH 15 minutes or until heated through.
Makes 5 to 6 servings

Classic French Onion Soup

¼ cup (½ stick) butter
3 large yellow onions, sliced
1 cup dry white wine
3 cans (about 14 ounces each) beef or chicken broth
1 teaspoon Worcestershire sauce
½ teaspoon salt
½ teaspoon dried thyme
4 slices French bread, toasted
1 cup (4 ounces) shredded Swiss cheese
    Fresh thyme sprigs

1. Melt butter in large skillet over medium-high heat. Add onions; cook and stir 15 minutes or until onions are soft and lightly browned. Stir in wine. Combine onion mixture, broth, Worcestershire sauce, salt and thyme in slow cooker.

2. Cover; cook on LOW 4 to 4½ hours. Ladle soup into 4 bowls; top with bread slice and cheese. Garnish with thyme sprigs.
Makes 4 servings

Creamy Turkey Soup

Double Thick Baked Potato-Cheese Soup

    2 pounds baking potatoes, peeled and cut into ½-inch cubes
    2 cans (10¾ ounces each) condensed cream of mushroom soup
1½ cups finely chopped green onions, divided
    ¼ teaspoon garlic powder
    ⅛ teaspoon ground red pepper
1½ cups (6 ounces) shredded sharp Cheddar cheese
    1 cup (8 ounces) sour cream
    1 cup milk
    Black pepper

1. Combine potatoes, soup, 1 cup green onions, garlic powder and red pepper in slow cooker. Cover; cook on LOW 8 hours or on HIGH 4 hours.

2. Add cheese, sour cream and milk; stir until cheese completely melted. Cover; cook on HIGH 10 minutes. Season to taste with black pepper. Garnish with remaining green onions. *Makes 7 servings*

Vegetable Medley Soup

    3 cans (about 14 ounces each) chicken broth
    3 sweet potatoes, peeled and chopped
    3 zucchini, chopped
    2 cups broccoli florets
    2 russet potatoes, peeled and shredded
    1 onion, chopped
    1 stalk celery, finely chopped
    ¼ cup (½ stick) butter, melted
    1 teaspoon black pepper
    2 cups half-and-half or milk
    1 tablespoon salt
    1 teaspoon ground cumin

1. Combine broth, sweet potatoes, zucchini, broccoli, russet potatoes, onion, celery, butter and pepper in slow cooker.

2. Cover; cook on LOW 8 to 10 hours or on HIGH 4 to 5 hours.

3. Add half-and-half, salt and cumin. Cover; cook 30 minutes to 1 hour or until heated through. *Makes 12 servings*

Double Thick Baked Potato-Cheese Soup

Potato & Spinach Soup with Gouda

 9 medium Yukon Gold potatoes, peeled and cubed (about 6 cups)
 2 cans (about 14 ounces each) chicken broth
 ½ cup water
 1 small red onion, finely chopped
 5 ounces baby spinach
 ½ teaspoon salt
 ¼ teaspoon ground red pepper
 ¼ teaspoon black pepper
2½ cups shredded smoked Gouda cheese, divided
 1 can (12 ounces) evaporated milk
 1 tablespoon olive oil
 4 cloves garlic, cut into thin slices
 5 to 7 parsley sprigs, finely chopped

1. Combine potatoes, broth, water, onion, spinach, salt, red pepper and black pepper in 4-quart slow cooker.

2. Cover; cook on LOW 10 hours or until potatoes are tender.

3. Slightly mash potatoes in slow cooker; add 2 cups Gouda and evaporated milk. Cover; cook on HIGH 15 to 20 minutes or until cheese is melted.

4. Heat oil in small skillet over low heat. Cook and stir garlic until golden brown; set aside. Pour soup into bowls. Sprinkle 2 to 3 teaspoons remaining Gouda cheese in each bowl. Add spoonful of garlic to center of each bowl; sprinkle with parsley.

Makes 8 to 10 servings

Potato & Spinach Soup with Gouda

Red Bean Soup with Andouille Sausage

2 tablespoons unsalted butter
1 large sweet onion, diced
3 stalks celery, diced
2 cloves garlic, chopped
8 cups chicken broth
1 ham hock
1½ cups dried red kidney beans, soaked in cold water 1 hour,
    drained and rinsed
1 bay leaf
2 parsnips, diced
1 sweet potato, diced
1 pound andouille smoked sausage or other smoked pork sausage,
    cut into ½-inch pieces
Salt and black pepper

1. Melt butter in large saucepan over medium heat. Add onion, celery and garlic; cook and stir 5 minutes. Place in 5- or 6-quart slow cooker. Add broth, ham hock, kidney beans and bay leaf. Cover; cook on HIGH 2 hours.

2. Remove ham hock and discard. Add parsnips and sweet potato. Cover; cook on HIGH 2 hours.

3. Add sausage. Cover; cook on HIGH 30 minutes or until heated through. Remove and discard bay leaf. Season with salt and pepper. *Makes 6 to 8 servings*

Red Bean Soup with Andouille Sausage

Chicken and Vegetable Chowder

1 pound boneless skinless chicken breasts, cut into 1-inch pieces
1 can (about 14 ounces) chicken broth
1 can (10¾ ounces) condensed cream of potato soup, undiluted
1 package (10 ounces) frozen broccoli florets, thawed
1 cup sliced carrots
1 jar (4½ ounces) sliced mushrooms, drained
½ cup chopped onion
½ cup corn
2 cloves garlic, minced
½ teaspoon dried thyme
⅓ cup half-and-half

1. Combine chicken, broth, soup, broccoli, carrots, mushrooms, onion, corn, garlic and thyme in slow cooker; mix well.

2. Cover; cook on LOW 5 to 6 hours.

3. Stir in half-and-half. Cover; cook on HIGH 15 minutes or until heated through.

Makes 6 servings

Variation: Add ½ cup (2 ounces) shredded Swiss or Cheddar cheese just before serving, stirring over LOW heat until melted.

Chicken and Vegetable Chowder

Pasta Fagioli Soup

       2 cans (about 14 ounces each) beef broth
       1 can (about 15 ounces) Great Northern beans, rinsed and drained
       1 can (about 14 ounces) diced tomatoes, undrained
       2 medium zucchini, quartered lengthwise and sliced
       1 tablespoon olive oil
    1½ teaspoons minced garlic
       ½ teaspoon dried basil
       ½ teaspoon dried oregano
       ½ cup uncooked tubetti, ditali or small shell pasta
       ½ cup garlic seasoned croutons
       ½ cup grated Asiago or Romano cheese
       3 tablespoons chopped fresh basil or Italian parsley (optional)

1. Combine broth, beans, tomatoes, zucchini, oil, garlic, basil and oregano in slow cooker; mix well.

2. Cover; cook on LOW 3 to 4 hours. Stir in pasta. Cover; cook on LOW 1 hour or until pasta is tender.

3. Serve soup with croutons and cheese. Garnish with fresh basil.

Makes 5 to 6 servings

Prep Time: 12 minutes
Cook Time: 4 to 5 hours

Helpful Hint

Only small pasta varieties like tubetti, ditali or small shell-shaped pasta should be used in this recipe. The low heat of a slow cooker will not allow larger pasta to completely cook.

Pasta Fagioli Soup

Farmhouse Ham and Vegetable Chowder

**2 cans (10¾ ounces each) condensed cream of celery soup,
    undiluted**
2 cups diced cooked ham
1 package (10 ounces) frozen corn, thawed
1 large baking potato, cut into ½-inch pieces
1 medium red bell pepper, diced
½ teaspoon dried thyme
2 cups small broccoli florets
½ cup milk

1. Combine soup, ham, corn, potato, bell pepper and thyme in slow cooker; mix well.

2. Cover; cook on LOW 6 to 8 hours or on HIGH 3 to 4 hours.

3. Stir in broccoli and milk. Cover; cook on HIGH 15 to 30 minutes or until broccoli is crisp-tender. *Makes 6 servings*

Easy Italian Vegetable Soup

1 can (about 14 ounces) diced tomatoes, undrained
1 can (10½ ounces) condensed beef broth
1 package (8 ounces) sliced mushrooms
1 medium yellow onion, chopped
1 medium zucchini, thinly sliced
1 medium green bell pepper, chopped
⅓ cup dry red wine or beef broth
1½ tablespoons dried basil
2½ teaspoons sugar
1 tablespoon olive oil
½ teaspoon salt
1 cup (4 ounces) shredded Mozzarella cheese (optional)

1. Combine tomatoes, broth, mushrooms, onion, zucchini, bell pepper, wine, basil and sugar in slow cooker.

2. Cover; cook on LOW 8 hours or on HIGH 4 hours. Stir oil and salt into soup. Garnish with cheese. *Makes 5 to 6 servings*

Farmhouse Ham and Vegetable Chowder

Hamburger Soup

1 pound ground beef
1 cup sliced celery
1 cup thinly sliced carrots
1 package (1 ounce) dry onion soup mix
1 package (1 ounce) Italian salad dressing mix
¼ teaspoon seasoned salt
¼ teaspoon black pepper
3 cups boiling water
1 can (about 14 ounces) diced tomatoes, undrained
1 can (8 ounces) tomato sauce
1 tablespoon soy sauce
2 cups cooked macaroni
¼ cup grated Parmesan cheese
2 tablespoons chopped fresh parsley

1. Brown beef 6 to 8 minutes in large skillet over medium-high heat, stirring to break up meat. Drain fat. Place celery and carrots in slow cooker. Top with beef, soup mix, salad dressing mix, seasoned salt and pepper. Add water, tomatoes, tomato sauce and soy sauce.

2. Cover; cook on LOW 6 to 8 hours.

3. Stir in macaroni and cheese. Cover; cook on HIGH 15 to 30 minutes or until heated through. Sprinkle with parsley just before serving.   *Makes 6 to 8 servings*

Hamburger Soup

Rustic Vegetable Soup

1 to 2 baking potatoes, cut in ½-inch pieces
1 jar (16 ounces) picante sauce
1 package (10 ounces) frozen mixed vegetables, thawed
1 package (10 ounces) frozen cut green beans, thawed
1 can (10½ ounces) condensed beef broth, undiluted
1 medium green bell pepper, chopped
½ teaspoon sugar
¼ cup finely chopped fresh parsley

1. Combine potatoes, picante sauce, mixed vegetables, green beans, broth, pepper and sugar in slow cooker.

2. Cover; cook on LOW 8 hours or on HIGH 4 hours. Stir in parsley.

Makes 8 servings

Potato-Crab Chowder

1 package (10 ounces) frozen corn, thawed
1 cup frozen hash brown potatoes, thawed
¾ cup finely chopped carrots
1 teaspoon dried thyme
¾ teaspoon garlic-pepper
3 cups chicken broth
½ cup water
1 cup evaporated milk
3 tablespoons cornstarch
1 can (6 ounces) crabmeat, drained
½ cup sliced green onions

1. Place corn, potatoes and carrots in slow cooker. Sprinkle with thyme and garlic-pepper. Add broth and water.

2. Cover; cook on LOW 4 to 5 hours.

3. Blend evaporated milk and cornstarch until smooth. Stir into slow cooker. Cover; cook on HIGH 15 to 30 minutes. Just before serving, stir in crabmeat and green onions.

Makes 5 servings

Rustic Vegetable Soup

Fiesta Black Bean Soup

> **6 cups chicken broth**
> **12 ounces potatoes, peeled and diced**
> **1 can (about 15 ounces) black beans, rinsed and drained**
> **½ pound cooked ham, diced**
> **½ onion, diced**
> **1 can (4 ounces) chopped jalapeño peppers**
> **2 cloves garlic, minced**
> **2 teaspoons dried oregano**
> **1½ teaspoons dried thyme**
> **1 teaspoon ground cumin**
> **Toppings: sour cream, chopped bell pepper and chopped tomatoes**

1. Combine broth, potatoes, beans, ham, onion, jalapeño peppers, garlic, oregano, thyme and cumin in slow cooker; mix well.

2. Cover; cook on LOW 8 to 10 hours or on HIGH 4 to 5 hours. Serve with desired toppings. *Makes 6 to 8 servings*

Vegetable and Red Lentil Soup

> **1 can (about 14 ounces) vegetable broth**
> **1 can (about 14 ounces) diced tomatoes, undrained**
> **2 medium zucchini or yellow summer squash (or 1 of each), diced**
> **1 red or yellow bell pepper, diced**
> **½ cup thinly sliced carrots**
> **½ cup red lentils, sorted and rinsed***
> **½ teaspoon salt**
> **½ teaspoon sugar**
> **¼ teaspoon black pepper**
> **2 tablespoons chopped fresh basil or thyme**

If you have difficulty finding red lentils, substitute brown lentils.

1. Coat slow cooker with cooking spray. Combine broth, tomatoes, squash, bell pepper, carrots, lentils, salt, sugar and pepper in slow cooker; mix well.

2. Cover; cook on LOW 8 hours or on HIGH 4 hours, or until lentils and vegetables are tender. Ladle into shallow bowls; top with basil. *Makes 4 servings*

Fiesta Black Bean Soup

Homestyle Chilis

Great Chili

    1½ pounds ground beef
    1½ cups chopped onion
      1 cup chopped green bell pepper
      2 cloves garlic, minced
      3 cans (about 15 ounces each) dark red kidney beans,
          rinsed and drained
      2 cans (about 15 ounces each) tomato sauce
      1 can (about 14 ounces) diced tomatoes, undrained
      2 to 3 teaspoons chili powder
      1 to 2 teaspoons dry hot mustard
    ¾ teaspoon dried basil
    ½ teaspoon black pepper
      1 to 2 dried hot chili peppers (optional)

1. Cook and stir ground beef, onion, bell pepper and garlic in large skillet until meat is browned and onion is tender. Drain fat. Place beef mixture in 5-quart slow cooker.

2. Add beans, tomato sauce, tomatoes, chili powder, mustard, basil, black pepper and chili pepper, if desired; mix well.

3. Cover; cook on LOW 8 to 10 hours or on HIGH 4 to 5 hours. Remove chili pepper, if desired, before serving.   *Makes 6 servings*

Great Chili

1-2-3 Chili

2 pounds ground beef
4 cans (about 8 ounces each) tomato sauce
3 cans (about 15 ounces each) chili beans in mild or spicy sauce,
**   undrained**
Shredded Cheddar cheese
Sliced green onions

1. Brown beef 6 to 8 minutes in large nonstick skillet over medium-high heat, stirring to break up meat. Drain fat. Combine beef, tomato sauce and beans with sauce in slow cooker; mix well.

2. Cover; cook on LOW 6 to 8 hours. Serve with cheese and green onions.

Makes 8 servings

Chicken and Black Bean Chili

1 pound boneless skinless chicken thighs, cut into 1-inch chunks
1 can (about 14 ounces) diced tomatoes, undrained
1 green bell pepper, diced
1 cup chunky salsa
1 small onion, chopped
3 cloves garlic, minced
2 teaspoons ground cumin
2 teaspoons chili powder
¾ teaspoon salt
1 can (about 16 ounces) black beans, rinsed and drained
**   Toppings: sour cream, diced avocado, shredded Cheddar cheese,**
**   sliced green onions or chopped cilantro, crushed tortilla chips or**
**   corn chips**

1. Coat slow cooker with cooking spray. Combine chicken, tomatoes, pepper, salsa, onion, garlic, cumin, chili powder and salt in slow cooker; mix well.

2. Cover; cook on LOW 5 to 6 hours or on HIGH 2½ to 3 hours or until chicken is tender.

3. Turn heat to HIGH; stir in beans. Cover; cook 5 to 10 minutes or until beans are heated through. Ladle into bowls; serve with desired toppings.   *Makes 4 servings*

1-2-3 Chili

Double-Hearty, Double-Quick Veggie Chili

2 cans (about 15 ounces each) dark kidney beans, rinsed and drained
2 bell peppers, chopped
1 small onion, chopped
1 can (about 14 ounces) diced tomatoes with peppers, celery and onions
1 cup frozen corn, thawed
3 tablespoons chili powder
2 teaspoons sugar
2 teaspoons ground cumin, divided
1 tablespoon olive oil
½ teaspoon salt
Sour cream
Chopped fresh cilantro

1. Combine beans, bell peppers, tomatoes, corn, chili powder, sugar and 1½ teaspoons cumin in slow cooker; mix well.

2. Cover; cook on LOW 6 hours or on HIGH 3 hours. Stir in oil, salt and remaining ½ teaspoon cumin. Serve with sour cream and cilantro.

Makes 4 to 6 servings

Double-Hearty, Double-Quick Veggie Chili

Chunky Chili

    1 pound ground beef
    1 medium onion, chopped
    2 cans (about 14 ounces each) diced tomatoes, undrained
    1 can (about 15 ounces) pinto beans, rinsed and drained
    ½ cup prepared salsa
    1 tablespoon chili powder
    1½ teaspoons ground cumin
    Salt and black pepper
    Toppings: shredded Cheddar cheese, sour cream and sliced black olives

1. Cook and stir beef and onion in large skillet over medium-high heat until beef is browned and onion is tender. Drain fat. Place beef mixture, tomatoes, beans, salsa, chili powder and cumin in slow cooker; stir.

2. Cover; cook on LOW 5 to 6 hours or until flavors are blended and chili is bubbly. Season with salt and pepper to taste. Serve with cheese, sour cream and olives.

Makes 4 servings

Black and White Chili

    Nonstick cooking spray
    1 pound chicken tenders, cut into ¾-inch pieces
    1 cup coarsely chopped onion
    1 can (about 15 ounces) Great Northern beans, drained
    1 can (about 15 ounces) black beans, drained
    1 can (about 14 ounces) Mexican-style stewed tomatoes, undrained
    2 tablespoons Texas-style chili powder seasoning mix

1. Spray large saucepan with cooking spray; heat over medium heat. Add chicken and onion; cook and stir 5 minutes or until chicken is browned. Combine chicken mixture, beans, tomatoes with juice and chili seasoning in slow cooker.

2. Cover; cook on LOW 4 to 4½ hours.   *Makes 6 servings*

Serving Suggestion: For a change of pace, this delicious chili is excellent served over cooked rice or pasta.

Chunky Chili

Chili

3 pounds ground beef
2 cans (about 14 ounces each) diced tomatoes
2 cans (about 14 ounces each) chili beans, undiluted
2 cups sliced onions
1 can (12 ounces) corn, drained
1 cup chopped green bell pepper
1 can tomato sauce
3 tablespoons chili powder
1 teaspoon garlic powder
½ teaspoon *each* ground cumin and oregano

1. Brown beef in batches 6 to 8 minutes in large skillet over medium-high heat, stirring to break up meat. Drain fat. Place in 5-quart slow cooker. Combine diced tomatoes, beans, onions, corn, pepper, tomato sauce, chili powder, garlic powder, cumin and oregano in slow cooker; mix well.

2. Cover; cook on LOW 4 to 5 hours or until onions are tender.

Makes 6 servings

Chunky Vegetable Chili

1 medium onion, chopped
2 stalks celery, diced
1 carrot, diced
3 cloves garlic, minced
**2 cans (about 15 ounces each) Great Northern beans, rinsed
    and drained**
1 cup *each* water and frozen corn
1 can (6 ounces) tomato paste
1 can (4 ounces) diced mild green chiles, undrained
1 tablespoon chili powder
2 teaspoons dried oregano

1. Combine onion, celery, carrot, garlic, beans, water, corn, tomato paste, chiles, chili powder and oregano in slow cooker.

2. Cover; cook on LOW 5½ to 6 hours or until vegetables are tender.

Makes 6 servings

Chili

Easy Slow-Cooked Chili

2 pounds lean ground beef
2 tablespoons chili powder
1 tablespoon ground cumin
1 can (28 ounces) crushed tomatoes in purée, undrained
1 can (15 ounces) red kidney beans, drained and rinsed
1 cup water
2 cups *French's*® French Fried Onions,* divided
¼ cup *Frank's*® *RedHot*® Original Cayenne Pepper Sauce
Sour cream
Shredded Cheddar cheese

For added Cheddar flavor, substitute **French's® Cheddar French Fried Onions for the original flavor.*

1. Cook ground beef, chili powder and cumin in large nonstick skillet over medium heat until browned, stirring frequently; drain. Transfer to slow cooker.

2. Stir in tomatoes with juice, beans, water, *½ cup* French Fried Onions and ***Frank's RedHot*** Sauce.

3. Cover; cook on LOW for 6 hours (or on HIGH for 3 hours). Serve chili topped with sour cream, cheese and remaining onions.   *Makes 8 servings*

Prep Time: 10 minutes
Cook Time: 6 hours

Easy Slow-Cooked Chili

Three-Bean Turkey Chili

> **1 pound ground turkey**
> **1 small onion, chopped**
> **1 can (about 28 ounces) diced tomatoes, undrained**
> **1 can (about 15 ounces) chickpeas, rinsed and drained**
> **1 can (about 15 ounces) kidney beans, rinsed and drained**
> **1 can (about 15 ounces) black beans, rinsed and drained**
> **1 can (about 8 ounces) tomato sauce**
> **1 can (about 4 ounces) diced mild green chiles**
> **1 to 2 tablespoons chili powder**

1. Cook and stir turkey and onion in medium skillet over medium-high heat until turkey is no longer pink, stirring to break up meat. Drain fat. Combine turkey mixture, diced tomatoes, chickpeas, kidney beans, black beans, tomato sauce, chiles and chili powder; mix well.

2. Cover; cook on HIGH 6 to 8 hours.

Makes 6 to 8 servings

White Bean Chili

> **Nonstick cooking spray**
> **1 pound ground chicken**
> **3 cups chopped celery**
> **1 can (about 16 ounces) whole tomatoes, undrained and chopped**
> **1 can (about 15 ounces) Great Northern beans, drained and rinsed**
> **1½ cups chopped onions**
> **1 cup chicken broth**
> **3 cloves garlic, minced**
> **1 tablespoon plus 1 teaspoon chili powder**
> **1½ teaspoons ground cumin**
> **¾ teaspoon ground allspice**
> **¾ teaspoon ground cinnamon**
> **½ teaspoon black pepper**

1. Spray large skillet with cooking spray. Brown chicken over medium-high heat, stirring to break up meat. Drain fat. Combine chicken, celery, tomatoes, beans, onions, broth, garlic, chili powder, cumin, allspice, cinnamon and pepper in slow cooker.

2. Cover; cook on LOW 5½ to 6 hours or until celery is tender.

Makes 6 servings

Three-Bean Turkey Chili

Chili with Chocolate

1 pound ground beef
1 medium onion, chopped
3 cloves garlic, minced and divided
1 can (about 28 ounces) diced tomatoes, undrained
1 can (about 15 ounces) chili beans in mild or spicy sauce, undrained
2 tablespoons chili powder
1 tablespoon grated semisweet chocolate
1½ teaspoons ground cumin
½ teaspoon salt
½ teaspoon black pepper
½ teaspoon hot pepper sauce

1. Cook and stir beef, onion and 1 clove garlic 6 to 8 minutes in large nonstick skillet over medium-high heat, stirring to break up meat. Drain fat.

2. Place beef mixture in slow cooker. Add tomatoes, beans, chili powder, remaining 2 cloves garlic and chocolate; mix well.

3. Cover; cook on LOW 5 to 6 hours. Add cumin, salt, black pepper and hot pepper sauce during last hour of cooking. *Makes 4 servings*

Helpful Hint

The chocolate added to this chili pairs well with the onions, garlic and spices to contribute richness, but not sweetness.

Chili with Chocolate

Cajun Chili

1½ pounds ground beef
2 cans (15 ounces each) Cajun-style mixed vegetables, undrained
2 cans (10¾ ounces each) condensed tomato soup, undiluted
1 can (about 14 ounces) diced tomatoes, undrained
3 fully cooked sausages with Cheddar cheese (about 8 ounces),
**   quartered and sliced into bite-size pieces**
Shredded Cheddar cheese (optional)

1. Brown ground beef 6 to 8 minutes in large nonstick skillet over medium-high heat, stirring to break up meat. Drain fat. Place beef, mixed vegetables, soup, tomatoes and sausages in slow cooker.

2. Cover; cook on HIGH 2 to 3 hours. Serve with shredded Cheddar cheese, if desired. *Makes 10 servings*

Turkey Chili

20 ounces JENNIE-O TURKEY STORE® Extra Lean Ground Turkey Breast
1 cup diced onions
1 (10-ounce) package shredded carrots
2 green peppers, diced
2 zucchini, diced
2 yellow squash, diced
2 tablespoons chili powder
6 cups water
2 tablespoons HERB-OX® Beef Bouillon Granules
1 (28-ounce) can diced tomatoes
1 (24-ounce) jar salsa
1 (15-ounce) can black beans, drained and rinsed
1 (15-ounce) can kidney beans, drained and rinsed

Brown ground turkey in large pan coated with vegetable spray. Add vegetables to pan; cook about 5 minutes or until onions are tender. Place turkey, vegetables and chili powder in large slow cooker along with water, beef granules, diced tomatoes, salsa and beans. Cover; heat mixture on LOW for 4 hours. *Makes 20 servings*

Prep Time: 30 minutes
Cook Time: 4 hours

Cajun Chili

Vegetarian Chili

1 tablespoon vegetable oil
1 cup finely chopped onion
1 cup chopped red bell pepper
2 tablespoons minced jalapeño pepper*
1 clove garlic, minced
1 can (about 28 ounces) crushed tomatoes
1 can (about 15 ounces) black beans, rinsed and drained
1 can (about 15 ounces) garbanzo beans, rinsed and drained
½ cup corn
¼ cup tomato paste
1 teaspoon sugar
1 teaspoon ground cumin
1 teaspoon dried basil
1 teaspoon chili powder
¼ teaspoon black pepper
Sour cream and shredded Cheddar cheese (optional)

Jalapeño peppers can sting and irritate the skin. Wear rubber gloves when handling peppers and do not touch your eyes.

1. Heat oil in large nonstick skillet over medium-high heat. Add onion, bell pepper, jalapeño pepper and garlic; cook and stir 5 minutes or until vegetables are tender. Combine vegetable mixture, crushed tomatoes, black beans, garbanzo beans, corn, tomato paste, sugar, cumin, basil, chili powder and black pepper in slow cooker; mix well.

2. Cover; cook on LOW 4 to 5 hours. Garnish with sour cream and cheese.

Makes 4 servings

Vegetarian Chili

Easy Side Dishes

Peasant Potatoes

¼ cup (½ stick) butter
1 large onion, chopped
2 cloves garlic, chopped
½ pound smoked beef sausage, cut into ¾-inch slices
1 teaspoon dried oregano
6 medium potatoes, preferably Yukon Gold, cut into
    1½ to 2-inch pieces
  Salt and black pepper
2 cups sliced Savoy or other cabbage
1 cup diced roasted red pepper
½ cup shredded Parmesan cheese

1. Melt butter in large skillet over medium heat. Add onion and garlic; cook and stir 5 minutes or until onion is transparent. Stir in sausage and oregano; cook 5 minutes. Stir in potatoes, salt and black pepper; mix well. Transfer mixture to slow cooker.

2. Cover; cook on LOW 6 to 8 hours or on HIGH 3 to 4 hours. Add cabbage and roasted peppers during last 30 minutes of cooking.

3. Top with cheese before serving.

Makes 6 servings

Peasant Potatoes

Winter Squash and Apples

1 butternut squash (about 2 pounds), peeled, seeded and cut into 2-inch pieces
2 apples, cored and cut into slices
1 medium onion, quartered and sliced
1 teaspoon salt
½ teaspoon black pepper
1½ tablespoons butter

1. Combine squash, apples, onion, salt and pepper in slow cooker; stir well.

2. Cover; cook on LOW 6 to 7 hours or until vegetables are tender. Stir in butter just before serving.   *Makes 4 to 6 servings*

Variation: Add ¼ to ½ cup packed brown sugar and ½ teaspoon ground cinnamon with butter in step 3; mix well. Cook an additional 15 minutes.

Asparagus and Cheese Side Dish

1½ pounds fresh asparagus, trimmed
2 cups crushed saltine crackers
1 can (10¾ ounces) condensed cream of asparagus soup, undiluted
1 can (10¾ ounces) condensed cream of chicken soup, undiluted
⅔ cup slivered almonds
4 ounces American cheese, cut into cubes
1 egg

1. Combine asparagus, cracker crumbs, asparagus soup, chicken soup, almonds, cheese and egg in slow cooker; mix well.

2. Cover; cook on HIGH 3 to 3½ hours or until asparagus is tender.
Makes 4 to 6 servings

Winter Squash and Apples

Spinach Spoon Bread

1 package (10 ounces) frozen chopped spinach, thawed and
   squeezed dry
1 red bell pepper, diced
4 eggs, lightly beaten
1 cup cottage cheese
1 package (5½ ounces) corn bread mix
6 green onions, sliced
½ cup (1 stick) butter, melted
1¼ teaspoons seasoned salt

1. Lightly grease slow cooker with nonstick cooking spray; preheat to HIGH.

2. Combine spinach, pepper, eggs, cottage cheese, corn bread mix, onions, butter and salt in large bowl; mix well. Pour batter into slow cooker.

3. Cook, covered with lid slightly ajar, on HIGH 1¾ to 2 hours or on LOW 3 to 4 hours or until edges are golden and knife inserted into center of bread comes out clean. Loosen edges and bottom of bread with knife and invert onto plate. Cut into wedges.

Makes 8 servings

Mexican-Style Rice and Cheese

1 can (about 15 ounces) Mexican-style beans
1 can (about 14 ounces) diced tomatoes with jalapeño peppers,
   undrained
2 cups (8 ounces) shredded Monterey Jack or Colby cheese, divided
1½ cups uncooked converted long-grain rice
1 large onion, finely chopped
½ package (4 ounces) cream cheese
3 cloves garlic, minced

1. Lightly grease slow cooker with nonstick cooking spray. Combine beans, tomatoes, 1 cup cheese, rice, onion, cream cheese and garlic in slow cooker; mix well.

2. Cover; cook on LOW 6 to 8 hours. Sprinkle with remaining 1 cup cheese just before serving.

Makes 6 to 8 servings

Spinach Spoon Bread

Rustic Cheddar Mashed Potatoes

2 pounds russet potatoes, peeled and diced
1 cup water
⅓ cup butter, cut into small pieces
½ to ¾ cup milk
1¼ teaspoons salt
½ teaspoon black pepper
½ cup finely chopped green onions
½ to ¾ cup (2 to 3 ounces) shredded Cheddar cheese

1. Combine potatoes and water in slow cooker; dot with butter. Cover; cook on LOW 6 hours or on HIGH 3 hours or until potatoes are tender.

2. Beat potatoes with electric mixer at medium speed until well blended. Add milk, salt and pepper; beat until well blended.

3. Stir in green onions and cheese. Cover; let stand 15 minutes to allow flavors to blend and cheese to melt.   *Makes 8 servings*

Easy Holiday Stuffing

1 cup butter, melted
2 cups chopped celery
1 cup chopped onion
1 teaspoon poultry seasoning
1 teaspoon leaf sage, crumbled
½ teaspoon ground black pepper
3 tablespoons HERB-OX® chicken flavored bouillon
2 eggs, beaten
2 cups water
12 cups dry breadcrumbs

In large bowl, combine butter, celery, onion, spices, bouillon, eggs and water together. Add breadcrumbs and stir to blend. Place mixture in slow cooker. Cook on HIGH for 45 minutes; reduce heat to LOW and heat for 6 hours (or cook on HIGH for 3 hours).   *Makes 12 servings*

Prep Time: 10 minutes
Total Time: 3¾ to 6¾ hours

Rustic Cheddar Mashed Potatoes

Red Cabbage and Apples

    1 small head red cabbage, cored and thinly sliced
    3 medium apples, peeled and grated
    ¾ cup sugar
    ½ cup red wine vinegar
    1 teaspoon ground cloves
    1 cup crisp-cooked and crumbled bacon

1. Combine cabbage, apples, sugar, vinegar and cloves in slow cooker.

2. Cover; cook on HIGH 6 hours, stirring after 3 hours. Sprinkle with bacon.

Makes 4 to 6 servings

Bean Pot Medley

    1 can (about 15 ounces) black beans, rinsed and drained
    1 can (about 15 ounces) red beans, rinsed and drained
    1 can (about 15 ounces) Great Northern beans, rinsed and drained
    1 can (about 15 ounces) black-eyed peas, rinsed and drained
    1 can (about 8 ounces) baby lima beans, rinsed and drained
    1½ cups ketchup
    1 cup chopped onion
    1 cup chopped red bell pepper
    1 cup chopped green bell pepper
    ½ cup packed brown sugar
    ½ cup water
    2 to 3 teaspoons cider vinegar
    1 teaspoon dry mustard
    2 bay leaves
    ⅛ teaspoon black pepper

1. Combine beans, ketchup, onion, bell peppers, brown sugar, water, vinegar, mustard, bay leaves and black pepper in 3½- to 4-quart slow cooker; stir until well blended.

2. Cover; cook on LOW 6 to 7 hours or until onion and bell peppers are tender. Remove and discard bay leaves before serving. *Makes 8 servings*

Red Cabbage and Apples

Scalloped Potatoes and Parsnips

¼ cup (½ stick) plus 2 tablespoons unsalted butter
3 tablespoons all-purpose flour
1¾ cups whipping cream
2 teaspoons dry mustard
1½ teaspoons salt
1 teaspoon dried thyme
½ teaspoon black pepper
2 baking potatoes, cut in half lengthwise, then crosswise
    into ¼-inch slices
2 parsnips, cut into ¼-inch slices
1 onion, chopped
2 cups (8 ounces) shredded sharp Cheddar cheese

1. Melt butter in medium saucepan over medium-high heat. Stir in flour; cook and stir 3 to 5 minutes. Slowly whisk in cream, mustard, salt, thyme and pepper until smooth. Arrange potatoes, parsnips and onion in slow cooker. Add cream sauce.

2. Cover; cook on LOW 7 hours or on HIGH 3½ hours or until potatoes are tender. Stir in cheese. Cover; let stand until cheese is melted.   *Makes 4 to 6 servings*

Helpful Hint

Baking potatoes, sometimes referred to as russet or Idaho potatoes, have a high starch content, which helps potato slices in scalloped dishes hold their shape.

Scalloped Potatoes and Parsnips

Spanish Paella-Style Rice

2 cans (about 14 ounces each) chicken broth
1½ cups uncooked converted long-grain rice
1 small red bell pepper, diced
⅓ cup dry white wine or water
½ teaspoon saffron threads, crushed, *or* ½ teaspoon ground turmeric
⅛ teaspoon red pepper flakes
½ cup frozen peas, thawed
Salt

1. Combine broth, rice, bell pepper, wine, saffron and red pepper flakes in 2½-quart slow cooker; mix well.

2. Cover; cook on LOW 4 hours or until liquid is absorbed.

3. Stir in peas. Cover; cook 15 to 30 minutes or until peas are heated through. Season with salt. *Makes 6 servings*

Note: Saffron is a very expensive spice, which tints dishes a yellow color as well as flavors them. Turmeric is a less expensive spice that produces the characteristic color but not the flavor of saffron. When purchasing saffron look for saffron threads rather than ground saffron because the threads retain their flavor longer.

Variations: Add ½ cup cooked chicken, ham or shrimp or quartered marinated artichokes, drained, with the peas.

Prep Time: 10 minutes
Cook Time: 4½ hours

Spanish Paella-Style Rice

Cran-Orange Acorn Squash

3 small acorn squash
¼ cup plus 1 tablespoon instant brown rice
3 tablespoons minced onion
3 tablespoons diced celery
3 tablespoons dried cranberries
Pinch ground or dried sage
1 teaspoon butter, cut into small pieces
3 tablespoons orange juice
½ cup water

1. Cut off tops of squash and enough of bottoms so they will sit upright. Scoop out seeds and discard; set squash aside.

2. Combine rice, onion, celery, cranberries and sage in small bowl. Stuff each squash with rice mixture; dot with butter. Pour 1 tablespoon orange juice over stuffing. Stand squash in slow cooker. Pour water into bottom of slow cooker.

3. Cover; cook on LOW 2½ hours or until squash are tender.   *Makes 6 servings*

Tip: The skin of squash can defy even the sharpest knives. To make cutting easier, microwave the whole squash on HIGH 5 minutes to soften the skin.

Cran-Orange Acorn Squash

Sweet-Spiced Sweet Potatoes

2 pounds sweet potatoes, peeled and cut into ½-inch pieces
¼ cup packed dark brown sugar
1 teaspoon ground cinnamon
½ teaspoon ground nutmeg
⅛ teaspoon salt
2 tablespoons butter, cut into ⅛-inch pieces
1 teaspoon vanilla

1. Combine sweet potatoes, brown sugar, cinnamon, nutmeg, salt, butter and vanilla in slow cooker; mix well.

2. Cover; cook on LOW 7 hours or on HIGH 4 hours. Add butter and vanilla; stir to blend. *Makes 4 servings*

Spicy Beans Tex-Mex

⅓ cup lentils
1⅓ cups water
5 strips bacon
1 onion, chopped
1 can (about 15 ounces) pinto beans, rinsed and drained
1 can (about 15 ounces) red kidney beans, rinsed and drained
1 can (about 14 ounces) diced tomatoes, undrained
3 tablespoons ketchup
3 cloves garlic, minced
1 teaspoon chili powder
½ teaspoon ground cumin
¼ teaspoon red pepper flakes
1 bay leaf

1. Boil lentils in water 20 to 30 minutes in large saucepan; drain. Cook bacon in medium skillet until crisp. Remove to paper towels. Cool and crumble bacon. Add onion to skillet; cook until soft.

2. Combine lentils, bacon, onion, beans, tomatoes, ketchup, garlic, chili powder, cumin, red pepper flakes and bay leaf in slow cooker.

3. Cover; cook on LOW 5 to 6 hours or on HIGH 3 to 4 hours. Remove bay leaf before serving. *Makes 8 to 10 servings*

Sweet-Spiced Sweet Potatoes

Green Bean Casserole

2 packages (10 ounces each) frozen green beans, thawed
1 can (10¾ ounces) condensed cream of mushroom soup, undiluted
1 tablespoon chopped fresh parsley
1 tablespoon chopped roasted red peppers
1 teaspoon dried sage
½ teaspoon *each* salt and black pepper
¼ teaspoon ground nutmeg
½ cup toasted slivered almonds*

*To toast almonds, spread in single layer in heavy-bottomed skillet. Cook over medium heat 1 to 2 minutes, stirring frequently, until almonds are lightly browned.

1. Combine green beans, soup, parsley, red peppers, sage, salt, black pepper and nutmeg in 2½-quart slow cooker; mix well.

2. Cover; cook on LOW 3 to 4 hours. Sprinkle with almonds.

Makes 4 to 6 servings

Sweet Potato & Pecan Casserole

1 can (40 ounces) sweet potatoes, drained and mashed
½ cup apple juice
⅓ cup plus 2 tablespoons butter, melted, divided
½ teaspoon salt
½ teaspoon ground cinnamon
¼ teaspoon black pepper
2 eggs, beaten
⅓ cup chopped pecans
⅓ cup packed brown sugar
2 tablespoons all-purpose flour

1. Lightly grease slow cooker. Combine sweet potatoes, apple juice, ⅓ cup butter, salt, cinnamon and pepper in large bowl. Beat in eggs. Place mixture in prepared slow cooker.

2. Combine pecans, brown sugar, flour and remaining 2 tablespoons butter in small bowl. Spread over sweet potatoes.

3. Cover; cook on HIGH 3 to 4 hours.

Makes 6 to 8 servings

Green Bean Casserole

Mediterranean Red Potatoes

**3 medium red potatoes, cut in half lengthwise,
    then crosswise into pieces**
**⅔ cup fresh or frozen pearl onions
    Nonstick cooking spray**
¾ teaspoon dried Italian seasoning
¼ teaspoon black pepper
1 small tomato, seeded and chopped
2 ounces (½ cup) feta cheese, crumbled
2 tablespoons chopped black olives

1. Place potatoes and onions in 1½-quart soufflé dish. Spray with cooking spray; toss to coat. Add Italian seasoning and pepper; mix well. Cover dish tightly with foil.

2. Tear off 3 (18×3-inch) strips of heavy-duty foil. Cross strips to resemble wheel spokes. (See page 15.) Place soufflé dish in center of strips. Pull foil strips up and over dish; place in slow cooker. Pour hot water into slow cooker to about 1½ inches from top of soufflé dish.

3. Cover; cook on LOW 7 to 8 hours.

4. Use foil handles to lift dish out of slow cooker. Stir tomato, cheese and olives into potato mixture.   *Makes 4 servings*

Easy Side Dishes • 211

Mediterranean Red Potatoes

Risotto-Style Peppered Rice

1 can (about 14 ounces) chicken broth
1 cup uncooked converted long-grain rice
1 medium green bell pepper, chopped
1 medium red bell pepper, chopped
1 cup chopped onion
½ teaspoon ground turmeric
⅛ teaspoon ground red pepper (optional)
4 ounces Monterey Jack cheese with jalapeño peppers, cubed
½ cup milk
¼ cup (½ stick) butter, cubed
1 teaspoon salt

1. Combine broth, rice, bell peppers, onion, turmeric and ground red pepper, if desired, in slow cooker; mix well.

2. Cover; cook on LOW 4 to 5 hours or until rice is tender and broth is absorbed.

3. Stir in cheese, milk, butter and salt; fluff rice with fork. Cover; cook on LOW 5 minutes or until cheese is melted.   *Makes 4 to 6 servings*

Risotto-Style Peppered Rice

Orange-Spiced Sweet Potatoes

2 pounds sweet potatoes, peeled and diced
½ cup packed dark brown sugar
½ cup (1 stick) butter, cut into small pieces
1 teaspoon ground cinnamon
1 teaspoon vanilla
½ teaspoon ground nutmeg
½ teaspoon grated orange peel
Juice of 1 medium orange
¼ teaspoon salt
Chopped toasted pecans*

*To toast pecans, spread in single layer in heavy-bottomed skillet. Cook over medium heat 1 to 2 minutes, stirring frequently, until almonds are lightly browned.

1. Combine sweet potatoes, brown sugar, butter, cinnamon, vanilla, nutmeg, orange peel, orange juice and salt in slow cooker; mix well.

2. Cover; cook on LOW 4 hours or on HIGH 2 hours or until potatoes are tender. Sprinkle with pecans before serving, if desired.   *Makes 8 servings*

Risi Bisi

1½ cups converted long-grain white rice
¾ cup chopped onion
2 cloves garlic, minced
2 cans (about 14 ounces each) chicken broth
⅓ cup water
¾ teaspoon Italian seasoning
½ teaspoon dried basil
½ cup frozen peas
¼ cup grated Parmesan cheese

1. Combine rice, onion and garlic in slow cooker. Bring broth and water to a boil in small saucepan. Stir broth mixture, Italian seasoning and basil into rice mixture.

2. Cover; cook on LOW 2 to 3 hours or until liquid is absorbed.

3. Add peas. Cover; cook 1 hour. Stir in cheese.   *Makes 6 servings*

Orange-Spiced Sweet Potatoes

Garden Potato Casserole

1¼ pounds baking potatoes, unpeeled, sliced
1 small green or red bell pepper, thinly sliced
¼ cup finely chopped yellow onion
2 tablespoons butter, cut into small pieces, divided
½ teaspoon salt
½ teaspoon dried thyme
Black pepper
1 small yellow squash, thinly sliced
1 cup (4 ounces) shredded sharp Cheddar cheese
Chopped green onion

1. Place potatoes, bell pepper, onion, 1 tablespoon butter, salt, thyme and black pepper in slow cooker; mix well. Evenly layer squash over potato mixture; add remaining 1 tablespoon butter.

2. Cover; cook on LOW 7 hours or on HIGH 4 hours.

3. Remove potato mixture to serving bowl. Sprinkle with cheese; let stand 2 to 3 minutes or until cheese melts. Garnish with green onion.   *Makes 5 servings*

Rustic Potatoes au Gratin

½ cup milk
1 can (10¾ ounces) condensed Cheddar cheese soup, undiluted
1 package (8 ounces) cream cheese, softened
1 clove garlic, minced
¼ teaspoon ground nutmeg
⅛ teaspoon black pepper
2 pounds baking potatoes, cut into ¼-inch slices
1 small onion, thinly sliced
Paprika (optional)

1. Heat milk in small saucepan over medium heat until simmering. Remove from heat. Add soup, cream cheese, garlic, nutmeg and pepper; stir until smooth.

2. Layer one fourth of potatoes and one fourth of onion in bottom of slow cooker. Top with one fourth of soup mixture. Repeat layers three times.

3. Cover; cook on LOW 6½ to 7 hours or until potatoes are tender and most of liquid is absorbed. Sprinkle with paprika.   *Makes 6 servings*

Garden Potato Casserole

Delicious Desserts

Mixed Berry Cobbler

1 package (16 ounces) frozen mixed berries
¾ cup granulated sugar
2 tablespoons quick-cooking tapioca
2 teaspoons grated lemon peel
1½ cups all-purpose flour
½ cup packed brown sugar
2¼ teaspoons baking powder
¼ teaspoon ground nutmeg
¾ cup milk
⅓ cup butter, melted
Ice cream (optional)

1. Stir berries, granulated sugar, tapioca and lemon peel in slow cooker.

2. Combine flour, brown sugar, baking powder and nutmeg in medium bowl. Add milk and butter; stir just until blended. Drop spoonfuls of dough on top of berry mixture.

3. Cover; cook on LOW 4 hours. Uncover; let stand about 30 minutes. Serve with ice cream, if desired. *Makes 8 servings*

Prep Time: 10 minutes
Cook Time: 4 hours
Stand Time: 30 minutes

Mixed Berry Cobbler

Pumpkin-Cranberry Custard

1 can (30 ounces) pumpkin pie filling
1 can (12 ounces) evaporated milk
1 cup dried cranberries
4 eggs, beaten
Whole gingersnap cookies and whipped cream (optional)

1. Combine pumpkin, evaporated milk, cranberries and eggs in slow cooker; mix well.

2. Cover; cook on HIGH 4 to 4½ hours. Serve with gingersnaps and whipped cream, if desired. *Make 4 to 6 servings*

Pineapple Rice Pudding

1 can (20 ounces) crushed pineapple in juice, undrained
1 can (13½ ounces) coconut milk
1 can (12 ounces) evaporated milk
¾ cup uncooked arborio rice
2 eggs, lightly beaten
¼ cup granulated sugar
¼ cup packed light brown sugar
½ teaspoon ground cinnamon
¼ teaspoon ground nutmeg
¼ teaspoon salt
Whipped cream

1. Place pineapple, coconut milk, evaporated milk, rice, eggs, granulated sugar, brown sugar, cinnamon, nutmeg and salt in slow cooker; mix well.

2. Cover; cook on HIGH 3 to 4 hours or until thickened and rice is tender. Remove cover; stir until blended. Serve warm or chilled with whipped cream.
Makes about 8 servings

Pumpkin-Cranberry Custard

Peach-Pecan Upside-Down Cake

1 can (about 8 ounces) peach slices
⅓ cup packed brown sugar
2 tablespoons butter or margarine, melted
¼ cup chopped pecans
1 package (16 ounces) pound cake mix, plus
ingredients to prepare mix
½ teaspoon almond extract
Whipped cream (optional)

1. Grease 7½-inch casserole dish.

2. Drain peach slices, reserving 1 tablespoon juice. Combine reserved peach juice, brown sugar and butter in prepared casserole. Arrange peach slices on top of brown sugar mixture. Sprinkle with pecans.

3. Prepare cake mix according to package directions; stir in almond extract. Spread over peach mixture. Cover casserole. Make foil handles (see page 15). Place casserole in slow cooker. Cover; cook on HIGH 3 hours.

4. Use foil handles to remove casserole from slow cooker. Cool, uncovered, on wire rack 10 minutes. Run narrow spatula around sides of casserole; invert onto serving plate. Serve warm with whipped cream, if desired.   *Makes 10 servings*

Prep Time: 10 minutes
Cook Time: 3 hours

Peach-Pecan Upside-Down Cake

Baked Fudge Pudding Cake

    6 tablespoons unsweetened cocoa powder
  ¼ cup all-purpose flour
  ⅛ teaspoon salt
    4 eggs
1⅓ cups sugar
    1 cup (2 sticks) unsalted butter, melted
    1 teaspoon vanilla
      Grated peel of 1 orange
  ½ cup whipping cream
      Whipped cream or vanilla ice cream
      Chopped pecans, toasted*

To toast pecans, spread in single layer in heavy-bottomed skillet. Cook over medium heat 1 to 2 minutes, stirring frequently, until almonds are lightly browned.

1. Spray slow cooker with nonstick cooking spray. Preheat slow cooker to LOW. Combine cocoa, flour and salt in small bowl; set aside.

2. Beat eggs in large bowl with electric mixer on medium-high speed until thickened. Gradually add sugar, beating 5 minutes or until very thick and pale. Mix in butter, vanilla and orange peel. Stir cocoa mixture into egg mixture. Add whipping cream; mix until blended. Pour batter into slow cooker. Line slow cooker lid with paper towel, making sure it does not touch the pudding mixture.

3. Cook on LOW 3 to 4 hours. (Do not cook on HIGH.) Top with whipped cream and pecans.   *Makes 6 to 8 servings*

Note: Store leftover cake in a covered container in the refrigerator. To serve leftover cake, reheat individual servings in the microwave about 15 seconds. Or make fudge truffles: roll leftover cake into small balls and dip them into melted chocolate. Let stand until chocolate hardens.

Baked Fudge Pudding Cake

Pear Crunch

1 can (8 ounces) crushed pineapple in juice, undrained
¼ cup pineapple or apple juice
3 tablespoons dried cranberries
1½ teaspoons quick-cooking tapioca
¼ teaspoon vanilla
2 pears, cored and cut into halves
¼ cup granola with almonds

1. Combine pineapple with juice, pineapple juice, cranberries, tapioca and vanilla in slow cooker; mix well. Place pears, cut side down, over pineapple mixture.

2. Cover; cook on LOW 3½ to 4½ hours. Arrange pear halves on serving plates. Spoon pineapple mixture over pear halves. Top with granola.   *Makes 4 servings*

Banana-Rum Custard with Vanilla Wafers

1½ cups milk
3 eggs
½ cup sugar
3 tablespoons dark rum or milk
⅛ teaspoon salt
1 cup water
1 medium banana, sliced ¼ inch thick
15 to 18 vanilla wafers

1. Whisk milk, eggs, sugar, rum and salt in 1-quart casserole. Add rack to 5-quart slow cooker and pour water into slow cooker. Place casserole on rack.

2. Cover; cook on LOW 3½ to 4 hours. Remove casserole from slow cooker. Spoon custard into individual dessert dishes. Arrange banana slices and wafers evenly over custard.   *Makes 5 servings*

Pear Crunch

Steamed Pumpkin Cake

1½ cups all-purpose flour
1½ teaspoons baking powder
1½ teaspoons baking soda
 1 teaspoon ground cinnamon plus additional for garnish
½ teaspoon salt
¼ teaspoon ground cloves
 2 cups packed light brown sugar
½ cup (1 stick) unsalted butter, melted
 3 eggs
 1 can (15 ounces) solid-pack pumpkin
 Sweetened whipped cream (optional)

1. Grease 2½-quart soufflé dish or baking pan that fits into slow cooker.

2. Combine flour, baking powder, baking soda, cinnamon, salt and cloves in medium bowl; set aside.

3. Beat brown sugar, butter and eggs in large bowl with electric mixer on medium speed until creamy. Beat in pumpkin. Stir in flour mixture. Spoon batter into prepared soufflé dish. Fill slow cooker with 1 inch hot water. Make foil handles (see page 15). Place soufflé dish into slow cooker.

4. Cover; cook on HIGH 3 to 3½ hours or until toothpick inserted into center comes out clean. Use foil handles to lift dish from slow cooker. Cool on wire rack 15 minutes. Invert cake onto serving platter. Cut into wedges. Serve with dollop of whipped cream sprinkled with additional cinnamon, if desired.

Makes 12 servings

Serving Suggestion: Enhance this old-fashioned dense cake with a topping of sautéed apples or pear slices, or a scoop of pumpkin ice cream.

Prep Time: 15 minutes
Cook Time: 3 to 3½ hours

Steamed Pumpkin Cake

Pineapple Daiquiri Sundae

1 pineapple, peeled, cored and cut into ½-inch chunks
½ cup dark rum
½ cup sugar
3 tablespoons lime juice
Peel of 2 limes, cut into strips, plus additional for garnish
1 tablespoon cornstarch or arrowroot
Ice cream, pound cake or shortcakes
Fresh raspberries and mint leaves (optional)

1. Place pineapple, rum, sugar, lime juice, lime peel and cornstarch in slow cooker; mix well.

2. Cover; cook on HIGH 3 to 4 hours. Serve warm over ice cream. Garnish with raspberries, mint and additional lime peel. *Makes 4 to 6 servings*

Variation: Substitute 1 can (20 ounces) crushed pineapple, drained, for the fresh pineapple. Cook on HIGH 3 hours.

Warm Spiced Apples and Pears

½ cup (1 stick) unsalted butter
1 vanilla bean
1 cup packed dark brown sugar
½ cup water
½ lemon, sliced and seeds removed
1 cinnamon stick, broken in half
½ teaspoon ground cloves
5 pears, quartered and cored
5 small Granny Smith apples, quartered and cored
Ice cream, whipped cream, sponge cake or pound cake (optional)

1. Melt butter in medium saucepan over medium heat. Cut vanilla bean in half and scrape out seeds. Add seeds and pod to pan with brown sugar, water, lemon slices, cinnamon stick and cloves. Bring to a boil; cook and stir 1 minute. Remove from heat. Place pears and apples in slow cooker; pour lemon syrup over fruit and mix well.

2. Cover; cook on LOW 3½ to 4 hours or on HIGH 2 hours, stirring once. Serve with ice cream, if desired. *Makes 6 servings*

Pineapple Daiquiri Sundae

Peach Cobbler

2 packages (16 ounces each) frozen peaches, thawed and drained
¾ cup plus 1 tablespoon sugar, divided
2 teaspoons ground cinnamon, divided
½ teaspoon ground nutmeg
¾ cup all-purpose flour
6 tablespoons butter, cut into small pieces

1. Combine peaches, ¾ cup sugar, 1½ teaspoons cinnamon and nutmeg in slow cooker; mix well. Combine flour, remaining 1 tablespoon sugar and ½ teaspoon cinnamon in small bowl. Cut in butter with pastry blender or two knives until mixture resembles coarse crumbs. Sprinkle over peach mixture.

2. Cover; cook on HIGH 2 hours.   *Makes 4 to 6 servings*

Cherry Rice Pudding

1½ cups milk
1 cup hot cooked rice
3 eggs, beaten
½ cup sugar
¼ cup dried cherries or cranberries
½ teaspoon almond extract
¼ teaspoon salt

1. Grease 1½ quart casserole with nonstick cooking spray. Combine milk, rice, eggs, sugar, cherries, almond extract and salt in prepared casserole. Cover with foil. Add rack to 5-quart slow cooker; add 1 cup water. Place casserole on rack.

2. Cover; cook on LOW 4 to 5 hours. Remove casserole from slow cooker. Cool on wire rack 15 minutes. Serve warm.   *Makes 6 servings*

Peach Cobbler

Fruit & Nut Baked Apples

4 large baking apples, such as Rome Beauty or Jonathan
1 tablespoon lemon juice
⅓ cup chopped dried apricots
⅓ cup chopped walnuts or pecans
3 tablespoons packed light brown sugar
½ teaspoon ground cinnamon
2 tablespoons butter or margarine, melted
 Caramel ice cream topping (optional)

1. Scoop out center of each apple, leaving 1½-inch-wide cavity about ½ inch from bottom. Peel top of apple down about 1 inch. Brush peeled edges evenly with lemon juice.

2. Mix apricots, walnuts, brown sugar and cinnamon in small bowl. Add butter; mix well. Spoon mixture evenly into apple cavities.

3. Pour ½ cup water in bottom of slow cooker. Place 2 apples in slow cooker. Arrange remaining 2 apples above but not directly on top of bottom apples.

4. Cover; cook on LOW 3 to 4 hours or until apples are tender. Serve warm or at room temperature with ice cream topping, if desired. *Makes 4 servings*

Helpful Hint

Acidic lemon juice is brushed onto the cut surfaces of apples and pears to prevent them from discoloring when they are exposed to air.

Fruit & Nut Baked Apples

Coconut Rice Pudding

2 cups water
1 cup uncooked converted long-grain rice
1 tablespoon unsalted butter
Pinch salt
2¼ cups evaporated milk
1 can (14 ounces) cream of coconut
½ cup golden raisins
3 egg yolks, beaten
Grated peel of 2 limes
1 teaspoon vanilla
Shredded coconut, toasted*

*To toast coconut, spread evenly on ungreased baking sheet. Bake in preheated 350°F oven 5 to 7 minutes or until light golden brown, stirring occasionally.

1. Place water, rice, butter and salt in medium saucepan. Bring to a boil over high heat, stirring frequently. Reduce heat to low. Cover; cook 10 to 12 minutes. Remove from heat. Let stand, covered, 5 minutes.

2. Meanwhile, spray slow cooker with nonstick cooking spray. Add evaporated milk, cream of coconut, raisins, egg yolks, lime peel and vanilla; mix well. Add rice; stir until blended.

3. Cover; cook on LOW 4 hours or on HIGH 2 hours. Stir every 30 minutes. Pudding will thicken as it cools. Top with toasted coconut.   *Makes 6 servings*

Coconut Rice Pudding

Steamed Southern Sweet Potato Custard

1 can (16 ounces) cut sweet potatoes, drained
1 can (12 ounces) evaporated milk, divided
½ cup packed light brown sugar
2 eggs, lightly beaten
1 teaspoon ground cinnamon
½ teaspoon ground ginger
¼ teaspoon salt
   Whipped cream and ground nutmeg (optional)

1. Place sweet potatoes and ¼ cup evaporated milk in food processor or blender; process until smooth. Add remaining evaporated milk, brown sugar, eggs, cinnamon, ginger and salt; process until well blended. Pour into ungreased 1-quart soufflé dish. Cover tightly with foil.

2. Crumple large sheet (about 15×12 inches) of foil; place in bottom of slow cooker. Pour 2 cups water over foil. Make foil handles (see page 15). Transfer dish to slow cooker using foil handles.

3. Cover; cook on HIGH 2½ to 3 hours or until skewer inserted into center comes out clean. Lift dish from slow cooker using foil strips; transfer to wire rack. Uncover; let stand 30 minutes. Garnish with whipped cream and nutmeg.   *Makes 4 servings*

Steamed Southern Sweet Potato Custard

"Peachy Keen" Dessert Treat

 2 pounds fresh peaches (about 8 medium), sliced
1⅓ cups uncooked old-fashioned oats
 1 cup granulated sugar
 1 cup packed light brown sugar
⅔ cup buttermilk baking mix
 2 teaspoons ground cinnamon
½ teaspoon ground nutmeg

1. Combine peaches, oats, granulated sugar, brown sugar, baking mix, cinnamon and nutmeg in slow cooker; mix until well blended.

2. Cover; cook on LOW 4 to 6 hours.

Makes 8 to 12 servings

Poached Pears with Raspberry Sauce

 4 cups cran-raspberry juice cocktail
 2 cups Rhine or Riesling wine
¼ cup sugar
 2 cinnamon sticks, broken into halves
 4 to 5 firm Bosc or Anjou pears, peeled and cored
 1 package (10 ounces) frozen raspberries in syrup, thawed

1. Combine juice, wine, sugar and cinnamon sticks in slow cooker. Submerge pears in juice mixture.

2. Cover; cook on LOW 3½ to 4 hours or until pears are tender. Remove and discard cinnamon sticks.

3. Place raspberries in food processor or blender; process until smooth. Strain and discard seeds. Spoon raspberry sauce onto serving plates; place pears on top of sauce.

Makes 4 to 5 servings

"Peachy Keen" Dessert Treat

Chocolate Croissant Pudding

1½ cups milk
3 eggs
½ cup sugar
¼ cup unsweetened cocoa powder
½ teaspoon vanilla
¼ teaspoon salt
2 plain croissants, cut into 1-inch pieces
½ cup chocolate chips
Whipped cream

1. Grease 1-quart casserole. Whisk milk, eggs, sugar, cocoa, vanilla and salt in medium bowl.

2. Layer half of croissants, chocolate chips and half of egg mixture in prepared casserole. Repeat layers. Add rack to 5-quart slow cooker; pour in 1 cup water. Place casserole on rack.

3. Cover; cook on LOW 3 to 4 hours. Remove casserole from slow cooker. Serve warm with whipped cream.   *Makes 6 servings*

Chocolate Croissant Pudding

Cherry Flan

5 eggs
½ cup sugar
½ teaspoon salt
¾ cup all-purpose flour
1 can (12 ounces) evaporated milk
1 teaspoon vanilla
1 bag (16 ounces) frozen, pitted dark sweet cherries, thawed
Whipped cream or ice cream
Cherries and mint leaves (optional)

1. Grease slow cooker.

2. Beat eggs, sugar and salt in large bowl with electric mixer at high speed until thick and pale. Add flour; beat until smooth. Beat in evaporated milk and vanilla. Pour batter into prepared slow cooker. Place cherries evenly over batter.

3. Cover; cook on LOW 3½ to 4 hours or until flan is set. Serve warm with whipped cream. Garnish with cherries and mint leaves. *Makes 6 servings*

Prep Time: 10 minutes
Cook Time: 3½ to 4 hours

Cherry Flan

Luscious Pecan Bread Pudding

3 cups day-old French bread cubes
3 tablespoons chopped pecans, toasted*
2¼ cups milk
2 eggs, beaten
½ cup plus 2 tablespoons sugar
1 teaspoon vanilla
¾ teaspoon ground cinnamon, divided
¾ cup cranberry juice cocktail
1½ cups frozen pitted tart cherries

To toast pecans, spread in single layer in heavy-bottomed skillet. Cook over medium heat 1 to 2 minutes, stirring frequently, until almonds are lightly browned.

1. Toss bread cubes and pecans in soufflé dish. Combine milk, eggs, ½ cup sugar, vanilla and ½ teaspoon cinnamon in large bowl. Pour over bread mixture in soufflé dish. Cover tightly with foil. Make foil handles (see page 15). Place soufflé dish in slow cooker. Pour hot water into slow cooker to about 1½ inches from top of soufflé dish.

2. Cover; cook on LOW 2 to 3 hours.

3. Meanwhile, combine cranberry juice and remaining ¼ teaspoon cinnamon in small saucepan; stir in frozen cherries. Bring sauce to a boil over medium heat; cook about 5 minutes. Remove from heat. Stir in remaining 2 tablespoons sugar.

4. Lift soufflé dish from slow cooker with foil handles. Serve bread pudding with cherry sauce. *Makes 6 servings*

Luscious Pecan Bread Pudding

Acknowledgments

The publisher would like to thank the companies and organizations listed below for the use of their recipes and photographs in this publication.

Hormel Foods, LLC

Jennie-O Turkey Store®

Lawry's® Foods

National Pork Board

Reckitt Benckiser Inc.

Index

METRIC CONVERSION CHART

VOLUME MEASUREMENTS (dry)

$1/8$ teaspoon = 0.5 mL
$1/4$ teaspoon = 1 mL
$1/2$ teaspoon = 2 mL
$3/4$ teaspoon = 4 mL
1 teaspoon = 5 mL
1 tablespoon = 15 mL
2 tablespoons = 30 mL
$1/4$ cup = 60 mL
$1/3$ cup = 75 mL
$1/2$ cup = 125 mL
$2/3$ cup = 150 mL
$3/4$ cup = 175 mL
1 cup = 250 mL
2 cups = 1 pint = 500 mL
3 cups = 750 mL
4 cups = 1 quart = 1 L

VOLUME MEASUREMENTS (fluid)

1 fluid ounce (2 tablespoons) = 30 mL
4 fluid ounces ($1/2$ cup) = 125 mL
8 fluid ounces (1 cup) = 250 mL
12 fluid ounces ($1 1/2$ cups) = 375 mL
16 fluid ounces (2 cups) = 500 mL

WEIGHTS (mass)

$1/2$ ounce = 15 g
1 ounce = 30 g
3 ounces = 90 g
4 ounces = 120 g
8 ounces = 225 g
10 ounces = 285 g
12 ounces = 360 g
16 ounces = 1 pound = 450 g

DIMENSIONS

$1/16$ inch = 2 mm
$1/8$ inch = 3 mm
$1/4$ inch = 6 mm
$1/2$ inch = 1.5 cm
$3/4$ inch = 2 cm
1 inch = 2.5 cm

OVEN TEMPERATURES

250°F = 120°C
275°F = 140°C
300°F = 150°C
325°F = 160°C
350°F = 180°C
375°F = 190°C
400°F = 200°C
425°F = 220°C
450°F = 230°C

BAKING PAN SIZES

Utensil	Size in Inches/Quarts	Metric Volume	Size in Centimeters
Baking or	$8 \times 8 \times 2$	2 L	$20 \times 20 \times 5$
Cake Pan	$9 \times 9 \times 2$	2.5 L	$23 \times 23 \times 5$
(square or	$12 \times 8 \times 2$	3 L	$30 \times 20 \times 5$
rectangular)	$13 \times 9 \times 2$	3.5 L	$33 \times 23 \times 5$
Loaf Pan	$8 \times 4 \times 3$	1.5 L	$20 \times 10 \times 7$
	$9 \times 5 \times 3$	2 L	$23 \times 13 \times 7$
Round Layer	$8 \times 1 1/2$	1.2 L	20×4
Cake Pan	$9 \times 1 1/2$	1.5 L	23×4
Pie Plate	$8 \times 1 1/4$	750 mL	20×3
	$9 \times 1 1/4$	1 L	23×3
Baking Dish	1 quart	1 L	—
or Casserole	$1 1/2$ quart	1.5 L	—
	2 quart	2 L	—